BETTER MONEY MANAGEMENT

CW00762567

BETTER MONEY MANAGEMENT

A step-by-step guide to
making your money go further

MARIE JENNINGS

PIATKUS

© 1994 Marie Jennings

First published in 1994 by
Judy Piatkus (Publishers) Ltd of
5 Windmill Street, London W1P 1HF

First paperback edition 1994

**The moral right of the author
has been asserted**

*A catalogue record for this book is
available from the British Library*

ISBN 0–7499–1304–5
ISBN 0–7499–1305–3 (pbk)

Designed by Paul Saunders

Set in 10½ on 13 pt Monophoto Times by
Datix International Ltd, Bungay, Suffolk
Printed and bound in Great Britain by
Biddles Ltd, Guildford and King's Lynn

Contents

Acknowledgements

Writing this book has been a daunting experience, but it has had its moments of delight! The daunting moments were when I recognised the size of the undertaking ... to try to encourage the reader to scale the mountains of understanding such a complex, sophisticated and fast-moving industry. The delightful moments came when I asked for help – and received it, generously and unstintingly, from many without whose co-operation this book, very simply, could not have been written.

Help given from within the financial services industry came from Dr Julian Farrand (the Insurance Ombudsman), Godfrey Jillings (chief executive of FIMBRA, the regulator covering independent financial advisers), Brian Brown (former chief executive of TSB Trust Company and a member of committees within the regulatory structure) and Peter Hayes (an independent financial adviser). I am most grateful to them for their patience in reading the text and commenting on points of detail and interpretation.

I would also like to acknowledge the help of rising professionals Michael Keegan and Sue Hood (on behalf of younger readers), and Tony Hood representing mature adults. Their comments and suggestions were invaluable.

John Moysey – administrator of the Money Management Council, the UK's money education charity which I founded some ten years ago and which is still, today, the only such organisation operating in the UK to help consumers understand personal financial matters – was also generous in the time he gave to comment in detail on Part 3 of this book. I would like to express my personal thanks to him for the trouble he took.

In addition, many others helped to a large degree, in refining my thoughts and sorting out my priorities in relation to what should and should not be included in the book. These included many concerned in the regulatory structure, practitioners and executives in the regulatory organisations, in particular Gareth Marr and David Peffer of FIMBRA, and Martin Tuckwell of LAUTRO. I should like to record my appreciation of them, and to those in professional and trade associations whom I have always found most helpful. In particular in this context I should mention the Life Insurance Association (Barry Woolley and John Ellis), the Chartered Insurance Institute (David Bland and John Eden), the National Federation of Independent Financial Advisers (Garry Heath) and IFAP (Joanne Hindle), also the many journalists I know who work in this field in the national and specialist media. In addition I should mention my thanks to consumer specialists Jean Eaglesham, Gerry Lanchin, Jeremy Mitchell, Barbara Saunders and Helena Wiesner, also the Office of Fair Trading.

From the beginning to the end, too, I have kept in mind the members of an organisation with which I have had much to do over many years and of which I have the honour to be president, the National Association of Women's Clubs. This book is dedicated to their many thousands of members throughout the country, and also to those in the many other voluntary organisations in the UK who do so much, silently and effectively, to ensure that the fabric of our society retains its strength in these difficult days. I hope that they will find the book helpful and benefit as a result of reading it.

My patient editors Anne Lawrance and Carol Franklin deserve a special bouquet, for their thorough and painstaking work to refine the text so that you, the reader, will find the book an easy read.

Finally, no acknowledgements would be complete without mention of my husband, Brian Locke, who has held my hand and comforted me through the writing of many books. He knows well that writing a book is rather like having a baby – the inception and gestation periods are pleasant, the birth traumatic, even if, in the end, the author feels a sense of achievement. But that sense of achievement also belongs to many who helped in the process. And this book belongs to all those I have mentioned in this note of acknowledgement. I do hope that they like the final result of all their work.

Preface

I believe passionately in the importance of good money management. Why is this? Just look at these key facts and the reasons will become immediately evident.

- With the average annual salary standing currently at £16–17,000 per year, and the average working life still considered to be 40 years, it is likely that some £700,000 will pass through the average worker's hands during that time.

- Now consider that, hopefully, your income will be increasing over the years. It is not unreasonable, therefore, that £800,000 or more may well pass through your hands (and/or that of your family) over a working life.

- It has been shown – with good money management – that it should be easily possible to make your money go at least 10 per cent further.

- And, with prudent investment of at least some money during your working life you should be able to add, over time, significantly to your total resources.

- Whether or not your income is above or below the average, the principles remain the same. They apply to everyone, at every level.

- In addition, effective management of your savings and investments should help you to achieve a happier life with fewer money worries.

Isn't the effort to achieve such a result worth some time and trouble? And yet so many people shy away from talking about money, from considering it objectively, from giving it the half an hour a week (or the monthly equivalent) to help their resources to 'grow', and to avoid needless or careless waste.

My own interest in good money management goes back many years, from the time when, as a young woman in my very early twenties, I had responsibility for managing a company and recognised that, without good money management, it was like trying to push water up a hill – it just wouldn't go! Then, over the years, writing in women's magazines, dealing with letters from readers and the public in general, lecturing on the subject (including to passengers on a cruise liner by way of a working holiday for my son and me) and working on public affairs responsibilities in the financial services industry, all made me very aware of the need for simple information and practical advice on personal finance for the consumer. Unless you have the relevant information, understand it, and know where to get the help and advice you need, the system can't possibly work for you! I have tried to distil all the necessary information and put that knowledge, and my experience, into this book. In a few instances I cover the ground more than once, and this is because of the need to review a different perspective in the specific area.

This book aims to urge you to examine the benefits of good money management, and to help you achieve it. I hope you find it of practical help.

Marie Jennings

PART ONE

YOU AND YOUR MONEY

CHAPTER 1

The Money Jungle

These days, money matters more than ever. The use of a little time and care can help ensure that you maximise your money and what it can do for you. It can also help you to avoid making costly mistakes.

When considering your financial affairs, it is of vital importance to learn more about the financial services industry, and to understand certain key facts about it and its relevance to you. Arming yourself with knowledge of the trends which are emerging will certainly affect your future planning of your savings and investments, and hopefully improve the results you are able to achieve.

What, then, are the emerging trends?

- The first point to make is the almost inevitable trend for government promotion of 'self-help' in terms of personal finance. It is already being acknowledged in international monetary circles that no government, of a developed or developing country, will, in the foreseeable future, be able to pay for State health, State education and State pension programmes. In the UK we have already made some progress along this path so are ahead of the game by comparison with some continental and other countries.

- The second point is that the financial services industries are being made to change dramatically from their origins by national and international economic and other factors. Taking the insurance industry as one example, the present shape of the industry, and the services it provides, are very different from their seventeenth- and eighteenth-century origins. And more change is on the way.

- As in all areas of marketing, there are vogues and fashions in financial services, all of which have their day. In recent years we have seen the vogue of the 'branded' financial product. It is already felt, in some well-informed circles in the financial services industry, that such products have had their day. In ten years' time some commentators think that the concept of marketed products will have given way to the 'designed' mix of services to help you, as the consumer, to achieve your stated and agreed objectives. This is to be welcomed. It will, however, mean that it is even more important that you understand the role of money in your life.

- In the twenty-first century 'self-reliance' will be the key to good and effective money management. But, to gain the most benefit from this, you will need to understand the money scene and to know how to get the best from your advisers and the companies with whom you place your business, and with whom you trust your money.

Seeking help

The development of the financial services industry has been fast and furious. Technological innovations have added to the speed of change. New products are issued weekly. It is almost impossible for the layperson to keep up to date with the daily movements of the enormous range of financial products. An analogy might be the modern motor car. The ordinary driver can no longer 'seriously' service and maintain a modern car since the special tools, special setting techniques and specialist knowledge required are beyond all but the specialist. The same applies to investment.

Quite simply, you need to have your hand held by a salesperson or adviser to ensure that you are making the most of your resources and your opportunities. Perhaps even more important, they need to help you make sure you are avoiding pitfalls and problems where possible.

The pitfalls of not being well informed

A recent report from the Equal Opportunities Commission disclosed that 250,000 women had been sold personal pensions when they would have been better off remaining in the State earnings-related pensions scheme (SERPS).

Department of Social Security figures show that, in the 1988/9 tax year, personal pensions were sold to 63,000 women who had no earnings and, therefore, did not even qualify to make contributions to any pension schemes.

However, you must not simply hand over responsibility for your affairs to an adviser. You need to have enough knowledge yourself to make your partnership with your adviser work effectively, and you must always keep closely in mind the fact that the ultimate responsibility for getting the most for your money rests with you and you alone. This is the key to financial planning today. What you need to come to grips with is a clear understanding of just how much you know, what your priorities are, and what to expect from the use of selected options in terms of savings and investment. (See Part 3 for more information about this.) Above all, you need to be very clear about *what you don't know* and recognise that this is where you could be at risk!

As we have seen, the trends for the future underline how important it is for everyone to put good financial planning into effect. However, the general picture at the moment (from a recent survey commissioned by Scottish Amicable from researchers MORI in 1992) is that few people are interested in seeking advice about the different ways in which they might save money! Seventy-five per cent of people have not sought any advice in the past year. The majority of people say they feel they know little, if anything at all, about the advantages and disadvantages of the various methods of saving and investment available to them. Most people are ill informed about such things as the rates of income tax, the differences between simple investment products such as unit and investment trusts, even the meaning of the PAYE code!

All of this means that we are all at risk because we don't know enough, don't know whom to ask and the right questions to ask. The result is that we aren't getting anything like the return we could get from our money. The solution is in our own hands . . .

If you keep in mind the fact that you could add at least 10 per cent per year to your financial resources by simple and effective money management which needn't take up too much of your time, you will find this is a tempting objective at which to aim. And, who knows, you might be able to beat it handsomely?

How to use this book

This book is really planned as a type of 'route-map' to guide you through the savings and investments money maze.

The book has three parts. The first focuses on you and your money, guiding you through the money jungle, telling you how to know yourself, and where you stand with regard to your savings and investments. It then holds your hand through the tax maze, identifying for you the information you must have with regard to understanding investments and developing your investment strategy. The book also identifies some special situations which are faced by many people every day.

The second part concentrates on getting financial advice. It explains how the system works and tries to guide you, as the reader, in a straightforward manner, on the choosing of a financial adviser and how to work with him or her. Tricks of the trade are explained, also how to keep track of your money and what to do if things go wrong.

The third part gives you a series of short, succinct snapshots of some of the most popular options for your money, and their benefits. It also gives advice on particularly difficult aspects.

Finally, the book also includes checklists and other information of a practical nature, as well as a list of useful names and addresses.

Using the book as a route-map should make knowing where you stand that much easier, and it should help to clear some of the mystique from a subject which still is shrouded in too much mystery and élitist jargon. As a result you should be able to see positive results and recognise that your money is going further to help you achieve what you want from your life.

Always consider...

Remember that the money markets are changing all the time – rapidly. How well you understand the products involved, the way they work, and also the way you work, and the priorities you have as regards the money in your life, directly affect how well your money can work for you.

Remember, too, that the whole system of life is interdependent, so what is happening in relation to the government of the day, how developing countries are performing, stress and other problems, whether on a personal or even a national and/or international dimension, do affect what happens to your money – and your life.

Whether your resources are slender or substantial, understanding money better will help you to get better value from it. The following tips and checklists will help you on your way.

Picking winners

Anyone with a foolproof technique for picking winners and avoiding losers in the financial services industry should be a multi-millionaire. It is a particularly difficult business. Here, however, are some tips which should be useful and provide a path to follow.

- **Do** find out as much as you can about how any system works and any adviser and/or the company before you take a decision. This book should help in your research.

- **Do** ask, and do try to ensure you know and understand the track record, past performance and perhaps future aspirations of your adviser, the company and/or the particular investment. It may be difficult but it is by no means impossible to get a reasonably good picture.

- **Do** understand the difference between the sales and advice functions of your adviser. If the advice is really there to underpin the sale of a specific product or range of products, do recognise that this is the priority. If the advice is given priority and the choice of product or investment is to enable that advice to be implemented to your advantage, then recognise that fact. If in doubt, ask the adviser and pin him or her down . . . preferably in writing.

- **Do** ensure you know what the penalties may be if you want to cash in your investment, your insurance policy or change course – you will need to know exactly what the cost is to you and what real return you have had for the time your money has been in that investment.

- **Do** ensure you know the level of risk you are being asked to take, and are comfortable with it.

- **Do** try to get independent endorsement of any advice before you take it.

- **Do** take time before you make a decision. Don't be rushed into one.

- **Do** calculate the likely return on your investment after taking inflation into consideration, and compare this with what you would receive from a bank deposit account.

The ten commandments of good financial management

1. Ensure you have made a budget and can 'make ends meet'.

2. Make sure you have a nest egg of 'rainy day' money to cope with an unexpected emergency – 6–9 months of a year's salary should be adequate.

3. Know where you stand with regard to savings and investments.

4. Know whether you are good, bad or indifferent in relation to your personal money management.

5. Know whether you can cope on your own, or whether you need the help of a financial adviser.

6. Know what you know about savings and investment and, more important, *know what you don't know!*

7. Know how to find out what you need to know about savings and investment, access to redress and/or compensation if you need them, also how to complain and to whom.

8. Ensure you have a good grip on your priorities to help you make the most of your money.

9. Ensure you know the right balance for you in relation to the 'mix' of savings and investment options you are comfortable with, and the proportion of these which will work for you in relation to security, income and growth opportunities.

10. Be aware of your attitude to risk and whether or not risky options are for you. Risks you may be asked to undertake include the fact that underlying investments may fall as well as rise in value; there may be no guarantees and a high annual return may be paid at the expense of depleting your capital; charges may be increased during the term of the investment; investment returns may be lower than projected when you bought; some of the investments may not be readily realisable and there may be delays built in before you can cash them.

The seven deadly sins in personal finance

1. Taking a flippant attitude to savings and investment.

2. Believing everything you are told by an investment adviser and not doing your own homework.

3. Giving someone charge of your financial affairs without checking him or her out carefully first.

4. Not taking the small amount of time and trouble necessary to plan ahead.

5. Not knowing your basic position on tax and as regards inflation.

6. Not being bothered to read the small print in an agreement you are asked to sign.*

7. Not taking the trouble to try to understand the basics of managing your money, and where to go for help and advice.

*In this context it is worth remembering two pieces of advice from the first Insurance Ombudsman: 'Ensuring that information given in a proposal form is complete and correct is far too important a job to leave to anyone else: check it carefully or you may be sorry!'

CHAPTER 2

Knowing Yourself

A recent Gallup Survey for Acuma (a former American Express company) revealed that one in four people said that they considered having 'copious amounts of money' more important than good health. And a staggering 40 per cent said that they considered money to be equal to or greater in importance than love or relationships. So it's obvious that many of us would jump at the chance of having more money! With good money management it is possible to make your money go that much further each year. And good money management starts with knowing more about yourself.

Looking at yourself – as a saver and investor

You may believe that you already know yourself, and your talents and abilities, that you have a good handle on life and can cope. You may consider that you are aware of your attitude to most aspects of your life, including money. But the question remains, do you really? And if you do, to what extent?

It is well worth spending time on the questions that follow. The answers you arrive at may surprise you. The process of self-analysis should lead you to a better understanding of how you handle money. And if you find yourself asking the question 'What money?' you have already identified an important factor that influences the sort of person you are where money is concerned.

Key questions to ask yourself

These are few and simple, but important. You need to think about them and work out your answers. The checklist and examples below should help.

- **Are you a spender or a saver by nature?**
  If you buy on impulse, spotting something you want and deciding that you *must* have it, then the chances are that you are a spender by nature. If, on the other hand, you are cautious, prone to making shopping lists and sticking to them, without adding any major 'extra' items, it is likely that you are a saver by nature.

- **Are you a good manager?**
  One way of looking at this is to review whether you decide to do things, and then go on and do them. If, on the other hand, you tend to take advice from others easily without checking out what they say, then the chances are that you are not a good manager!

- **Can you control your expenditures? Do you prepare a plan and stick with it?**
  To decide where you stand on this question, look back over the last two years. If you feel that there were no major items of expenditure you incurred that you hadn't planned, that you did not need to dig into your 'rainy day' money to cover costs for an unexpected major item, then you will know that, indisputably, you *are* a good planner and you *can* control your expenditures.

- **What are your objectives in life?**
  Do you want to be wealthy? Well known? Successful in your field? Happy? To have a satisfying home life?
  Here are some tips to help you to know where you stand.

  – Do you tend to talk a lot about money? If you do it generally indicates that money is important to you and that you want to be (or stay) wealthy.

- Do you tell others immediately if you have been praised or have achieved something? If you do you probably want to be well known and successful in your field.

- Are you on the look-out for publicity opportunities? This too can indicate that the approval of others is important to you in your search for success.

- **What is your attitude to money? Do you worry about it?**
Sleepless nights and stress, resulting in your being tetchy over small things, can indicate that you are worried about money and are over-anxious about how you are managing your money.

- **Would you say you are materialistic?**
If you put a value on everything and want to know the price of everything this generally indicates a materialistic turn of mind.

- **Do you ignore, or try to ignore, money matters?**
If you tend to put bills into a drawer unopened, and try to avoid speaking about money and reviewing your financial affairs, this can frequently be a sign of a future problem which can only grow if it is ignored over time.

- **What is your attitude to risk?**
Does risk frighten or worry you? Does it stimulate you? Do you enjoy taking risks in life, e.g. driving fast cars?
    If you try to avoid the unknown and want always to know where you stand, this indicates that you are 'risk averse'.

- **What is your attitude to stress?**
Can you cope with stress? A recent survey by Acuma established that one-third of interviewees claimed to be suffering from 'money stress' and one in five are actually not sleeping over worrying about their finances! Does this include you?

Answering these questions frankly simply means that you will get to know yourself that much better – and this is essential ammunition to help you to manage your finances well and choose the right sort of investments. On the one hand you should get the measure of what you need to know in the area of savings and investments, on the other you may feel much more comfortable with taking decisions and asking for the help of experts by reason of recognising how much you do know about the subject. The following 'profiles' may help you even further.

Identify yourself

A few years ago the Midland Bank undertook a series of research projects to find out how women handle money. They discovered that women fitted into four basic categories, but the types they identified cover men equally well. They are as follows.

Type A: The competents

These are people who are capable and who care about good money management. They are characterised by the fact that they already have expertise in financial matters, and are enthusiastic about learning how to manage money effectively and do it well. They plan ahead and recognise the need to make good decisions at the right time to maximise opportunities and contain likely problems. They have a detailed knowledge of what to expect over the next year and also a broad idea of where they will expect to be in five years' time. They keep in touch with the fast-moving financial scene through reading the financial pages in the national media. Most of them would be aware of the different financial products and services, and the nature of the financial advice available to them.

Many of them would not be completely aware of the sophistication of financial marketing techniques used and could make mistakes as a result.

Type B: The triers

These people know quite a bit about money and may well develop to join the first group in time. They have, however, different priorities, perhaps in terms of home and family or work. They will make their own independent decisions, including financial decisions, but financial matters have to take their turn in their list of priorities. As a result they could well be at risk.

Because they do have some spare money and need, when they think about it, to ensure that they are putting this to good use, the triers are all too often open-minded when the voracious salesperson calls, or when the attractive brochure or persuasive letter pops through the letter-box. They, too, are well targeted by the financial industry's marketing machine. They could easily make mistakes by not being certain what they really need or want.

Type C: The copers

These are those people who, while not being poor in the accepted sense of that word, are overburdened with worries, pressures and other priorities. They try to cope but are often over-tired and over-stressed. As a result they, too, could well be at risk. The chances are that they don't believe they have the necessary time to plan ahead and they are less well informed than the first two groups as a result. The persuasion machine can find them an easy target because they haven't planned ahead, don't know what they have got and haven't thought of the possible dangers facing them in the years to come as a result of this lack of planning. In the terms of the financial services industry they are defined as 'naïve' – which conjures up a spirit of charm and freshness, but are seen by some salespeople as gullible and a 'soft sales target'. This group should remember that information is power and investor knowledge is the finest means of investor protection.

Type D: The casuals

These are the people who either don't bother to understand money or can't cope with it. They can include those without money and those with altogether too much, who spend it in the hope that someone will provide more if and when the money runs out! This group is perhaps the least at risk from the marketing machine, but perhaps it is the group most at risk from itself!

Setting your basic objectives

Setting objectives in your life is important. It shouldn't be seen as a chore, and indeed you could find it fun. But it is a critically important process if you are serious about getting that extra 10 per cent from your money.

The questions to be answered are not many, but it is important for you to know your answers to them. Ask yourself these questions.

1. Do you know what your basic financial situation is?

2. Are you currently living within your means?

3. Are you a saver or a spender by nature? (The extent of any possible susceptibility to overspending needs to be identified.)

4. What are your commitments? This is an essential first step to prudent savings and investments, and will be covered in detail in Chapter 3.

5. Can you identify the groups of people that are important to you among your family, friends and the people you work with? Do you recognise the responsibilities you have to them, particularly those with financial implications? For example, if you have children, your responsibility to them includes looking after them financially until they have reached maturity. This needs to be quantified.

6. Do you have a picture of what the future should, ideally, hold for you? For example, look five years ahead and decide whether or not you wish to be in the same job, with the same home and surroundings, with a nice little nest egg of savings to help your money grow. In ten years' time, you should be able to know if you are travelling in the right direction or not, and whether or not this satisfies you. You will need to know that your financial responsibilities are

contained, that you are building up your nest egg, that you are knowledgeable about what lies ahead in terms of retirement or even building your own business. For example, you will be able to recognise just how much you may be able to manoeuvre with that important 'cushion' (your resources between income and capital resources, and expenditure/commitment), to meet longer term objectives which you will now be able to plan. And are you happy with the financial implications of all this?

7. Is security a major priority for you? This is an important question to answer. If you grasp opportunities then you will know that you are not risk-averse. If, on the other hand, you always want to keep your feet on the ground and avoid the unknown then you should recognise that security is a major factor for you and act accordingly. In this context you should bear in mind the tax planning implications. It may be possible for you to plan options which are more tax efficient – paying less tax is, after all, very much the objective for most people.

8. Are possessions important to you? To help you decide, just consider that you are being offered the chance to make a most attractive investment, but to do this you have to put up security, for example your home. Would you do it? And under what conditions would you consider such an action? By reflecting on your answers to these questions you will know whether or not possessions are important to you.

9. Is quality of life important? You can address this question by considering that you have an opportunity to take up an attractive and impressive new job – in another part of the country or in another country. Your current lifestyle pleases you and your family, you enjoy your home and your friends, and the area in which you live. Would you uproot the family or not? Your answer will reveal to you whether you put present quality of life above potential career development or making money.

10. Are you satisfied with your life? Do you feel fulfilled? Or do you wish to alter your life drastically? These are important

questions and are difficult to address, let alone answer. But if you sleep easily at night, do not feel unduly stressed or pressured, don't find yourself losing your temper over small matters, find that you have the time to remember those little things which others find important, such as birthdays and anniversaries, then the chances are that you are satisfied with your life, and a happy and lucky individual!

Ensuring you have the answers to these questions is most important. Why? Because when you have them you will be able to relax and get on with planning your life, knowing that the important financial implications have been thoroughly investigated and you know how to protect your ease of mind.

Thinking about risk

In any evaluation of your savings and investments and future planning, it is essential to know your attitude to risk. The subject of risk is central to the performance of all savings and investments. In basic terms the higher the risk the higher the reward: the lower the risk, the lower the reward, but the higher the security factor. Some may argue that this is not always the case, but it is a useful rule of thumb to start out with.

Risk features at the heart of the Financial Services Act 1986, the major piece of legislation affecting your savings and investments. The 'Know Your Customer' rules mean that your financial adviser should alert you to the level of risk you are being asked to take with regard to any savings and investment option you are considering, and make sure you feel comfortable with it. In practice the risk element – if it features at all – tends to be confined to the small print and/or the subject is likely to be glossed over by the adviser who is dealing with your case.

Risk is, of course, fundamental to all decisions we have to take in life. If, however, you are unsure as to your own attitude to risk then it is self-evident that you could be putting much which is important to you at risk.

It is important, too, to recognise that there are many different types of risk.

So, how do you define risk and how do you determine your attitude to it? How can it be related to your requirements with regard to your savings and investments?

As an example, let us assume that you have a reasonable cushion in relation to savings and investments, and you have opted for a relatively safe course by putting some of the money into unit trusts – the 'starter kit' to investments in equities, offering many opportunities to 'grow' your capital (see Part 3, page 157 of this book). Now you find that over the past few years the value of your particular unit trust portfolio has halved. What do you do? Do you take the money out and chalk it up to experience? Or do you leave the money in the unit trusts in the hope that the markets will recover what you have lost and then add value to your original investment? Or would you be so worried about what has happened that you just don't know what to do and to whom to turn?

The answers to that simple series of questions should help to determine your attitude to risk.

CHAPTER 3

Where Do You Stand?

Now you are armed with self-knowledge you need to assess where you stand financially. It is important to review what you have in terms of savings and investments right now, and whether some or all of this money is 'locked up' so that you can't get at it if you need it. Also, determine where any other money may be which is not 'locked up' and could be moved around if that is what you decide you want to do. And work out what is spare from your income which you could be putting to work for you.

The essential question you have to answer is 'Are you making the most of what money and other resources you have?' This means the raw material with which you have to work. To this basic resource you need to add any extra assets. You now need to prepare your own 'Wealth Check' to know where you stand.

It is important to stress that your aim should be to live within your income, at the same time setting aside as much as may be reasonable to help you build up a reserve, and to go towards any additional and special items of expenditure and/or emergencies which you may have to face. It is essential to ensure that you have some 'rainy day' money, and that you make provision for long-term savings and investments, pensions and the like.

Your 'Wealth Check'

To prepare your own 'Wealth Check' you must first of all look at your assets. These are items of value, large and small. At the top end they may include your home (even if you are still buying it on a mortgage), any life assurance policies and investments you may have, any pension contributions you have paid, your bank balance and your car. At the other end they include any items of jewellery, pictures, antiques or other valuables you may own. Your list of assets should also include a note of any expectations you may have related to property, money or valuables you might inherit, together with when they may come into your possession.

In listing your assets you should be careful to separate out what belongs to you, from what may belong to your husband, wife or partner; also what may be in joint ownership between you and someone else. For some of these items you will need to separate out the capital value from any income that the asset provides. Then, of course, you need to list your income in the year, in as much detail as possible.

On the other side of the coin, your 'Wealth Check' should include a list of your liabilities and any commitments. These can range from the mortgage on your home to the hire-purchase payments you may need to pay on the car; from the money you still owe for last year's holiday to the balances due on your credit card statements. Don't forget to include any bank over-draft you may have and money due on regular commitments, such as for the council tax, water rates, gas, electricity etc., over the year. Don't forget, too, that many liabilities involve regular interest payments as well as paying off the basic sums borrowed. Remember your tax levels as well.

Then, of course, you should include an estimate of your expenditure for the year, to include all living expenses.

So, what should you include on your 'Wealth Check'? On the page opposite is an example which you can adapt to suit your purposes – and remember, too, it could be useful for your household insurance details.

Assets less liabilities reflect your total wealth. If liabilities exceed assets you need to consider carefully how you would make repayments if you suffered a reduction in income, or had a sudden unexpected bill to pay or an unforeseen situation to make provision for.

Do take care not to mix up liabilities of a capital nature with any commitments out of income, e.g. insurance premiums.

Assets

Home (estimated value) (what it would sell for in today's market, less what is owed on mortgage) _____

Car (what it could be sold for) _____

Savings (building societies and bank accounts)
(surrender values of any relevant insurance policies – you would have to ask to receive this information) _____
(government stocks, shares, unit trusts and other securities) _____
(other forms of savings) _____

Tangible assets (including items of value, say over £500) _____

Jewellery and valuables (which could have a collectable value) (at what they would sell for) _____
Home contents (what they would fetch if sold, not what they originally cost – but you may need to have any valuable antiques or pictures valued separately) _____
Other (including any special insurances, pension plans etc.) _____

TOTAL ASSETS: _____

Liabilities

Mortgage/loans outstanding _____

Hire-purchase and/or shop credit debts _____

Overdraft or bank loans _____

Other outstanding loans _____

Insurances _____

Tax liabilities _____

Credit card balances to be paid off _____

Other debts and/or commitments _____

TOTAL LIABILITIES: _____

TOTAL WEALTH: _____

Schedule of needs

The next step is to prepare your own 'Schedule of Needs'. This will help to determine whether you should be planning for income or growth, and if you have to save for school fees, holidays and/or other future expenditures. You will be able to identify your requirements in the area of pensions, future security, inheritance tax planning etc.

To develop your own Schedule of Needs you need to balance several factors, which relate to the choice of specific investment needs. These in turn will be related to consideration, among other items, of:

- your individual needs and aspirations;

- how well these are currently satisfied;

- the level of safety you require – of both capital and income;

- the level of risks you are prepared to take;

- your assessment of the prospects and the alternatives.

You can take your decisions by hunch, from knowledge or research. But they can all be helped by access to reliable information. There are some key factors to consider when making these decisions, so you need to be very sure that you have armed yourself with the relevant information before the decision-making process begins.

Here is a basic Schedule of Needs which you can adapt to suit your purpose.

Need 1: PROTECTION (see Chapters 6 and 12)
You need to know that bills will be paid if you are ill for a long period or that your dependants will be looked after if you die prematurely. Solutions to these problems are reasonably cheap and are insurance-based.

What to look for

- If you are in regular employment and have not 'contracted out' of SERPS (see Glossary), check the benefits in your company pension scheme.
- Look into the possibility of taking out permanent health insurance.
- Take out term assurance and whole life assurance.
- Check up on State benefits as they affect you.
- Try to have a year's income available to you if you need it.
- Think also of insuring your partner's life, particularly if you have young children. (Term assurance can be particularly good value to cover death, but remember it has no material value.)

Need 2: SAVINGS

Lump sum cash is often needed to pay for special items, like the deposit on a new car or a holiday.

What to look for

- Keep some short-term savings readily available in a bank or building society account, as distinct from investments.

Need 3: YOUR HOME

You may choose to buy or to rent. Be realistic about the value of a house as an asset if you buy. Be realistic also as to the likely level of maintenance costs.

What to look for

- Recent events have led to the reappraisal of a home as a desirable investment – be clear on the nature and value of your home to you, whether it is bought or rented.
- If you have an endowment mortgage check up on its financial efficiency.

Need 4: WEALTH CREATION

Reserves are longer term savings – for retirement, for your children's future or for a major project some years ahead. You should not embark on this until you have satisfied yourself that you have adequately covered the first three priorities. You must be prepared to keep on saving for several years and, in many cases, accept the ups and downs in market values to get the best return over the longer term.

What to look for

The types of investment you will be looking for are:

- Life assurance policies of the savings type, endowment or unit-linked. These should be looked on as long-term investments of at least ten years, as early surrender will impose a significant financial penalty. Other options include unit and investment trusts (the starter-kit products for investment in equities) and equities themselves (stocks and shares).
- Finally there are pensions: State, company and personal pension schemes.

Different ages and different money needs

At various stages in our lives we have differing needs in terms of money and financial resources. Here are some examples.

The young

Young children and those up to their early teens naturally expect that their parents will provide for them. However, it is important that the money management habit is inculcated as early as possible. Value for money has to be taught, in terms of the value of time and the value of the money itself. Parents can help by providing pocket money allowances if possible and perhaps setting rates for help with household chores.

Teens and early twenties

At this time of life young people come up against many material temptations. The chances are that they have not learnt much about money management at school or at home. The true costs of goods – including the cost of credit – may well have eluded them. It is important for this group to develop the banking habit, perhaps having a National Savings or building society account in addition to a bank account. Now is the time, too, to explore the benefits of life assurance which can offer attractive rates at this early time of life.

If you are a member of this group you should be aware that, as first-time buyers, you are the darlings of the financial world. Everyone wants your custom and to recruit you as new, long-term customers. Rates can reflect this and therefore it is to your advantage to check up on your financial knowledge and soak up information like a sponge. At the other end of the scale you could be at risk if you are naïve and liable to be exploited by others. You need to create financial relationships – with your bank etc., to help you build your knowledge and experience of handling money well.

One facility which may appeal to young people is the ability to take out a 'Student Loan'. This is an advance funded by Government which is repayable when they are working and earning their own income in 'real terms'. The student seeking a loan makes an application to the Bursar at The Student Loans Company Ltd (see Appendix). The student completes an application form which is then used at any following interview. The form and information provided by the establishment following the interview are then considered to confirm whether or not the student has satisfied the criteria to get the loan requested. Career Development Loans are also available to help students borrow money for their courses under a partnership between the Employment Department and Barclays, the Co-operative and Clydesdale Banks. Under this scheme the Government pays the interest on a Career Development Loan while the student is still studying or training. And there's nothing to pay until up to three months after the course has been completed.

Young adults

This group, likely to be in their early twenties to early thirties, is the group with the greatest need to understand effective money management. These years are high-spending years with major new commitments in terms of costs of raising a family and of making a home, also the everyday costs of family life with holidays, children's clothes etc., eating into the family's financial resources. This is the time when the cost of credit needs to be understood, when it is essential to have adequate protection in terms of insuring against eventualities which could blow the family's financial ship off course, when it is critically important to understand the effects of good budgeting and to shy away from the disasters which can follow bad budgeting. This is also the time when it is important to put down some building blocks for the future, with life assurance and pension provision, and to start to come to grips with the financial implications of the years which lie ahead – even if they do seem very far away at this busy, energetic stage of life!

Mature adults

This group – from the early thirties to late forties – have perhaps had to learn from their mistakes at earlier stages in their lives. By now they should know whether they are good or bad at money management. By now they should recognise the importance of planning ahead for the years which will be following on. Priorities will be looking at pension provision, looking at whether or not a house move may lie in the future, when the children have grown up and left home, at whether financial insecurity could result from possible redundancy or early retirement as a result of possible adverse trading conditions, at whether you will be able to make ends meet. This is a time of life when you need to be brutally honest with yourself and look the future in the face. Now is the time to ensure that your planning is right for your particular circumstances and that any financial surprises are pleasant and not the reverse! Now is the time to ensure that you have sorted out your relationships with the money managers and are comfortable with them, that you know whom to ask and the questions to ask to ensure that your financial future is as secure as you can possibly make it.

The fifty-plus group

This is – or should be – a new 'third' age for you, a new beginning. With prudent forethought and planning in earlier years it is a time when you should be able to enjoy the easing of pressures, at work and at home. This is a time of diminishing financial commitments with, hopefully, more time for leisure activities which you can enjoy. These are the years which should contain fulfilment and a sense of relaxation as you enjoy the fruits of your labour over earlier years. At this time of life your confidence in your financial advisers should be there, simply because you have worked on getting your priorities right in earlier years.

In this context, too, it is important to recognise that in today's fast-moving world when you are even as young as your late twenties or early thirties, there is a need to ensure that effective pension planning is in place. This is particularly important if you are self-employed.

It is sad but true to recognise that in the high-spending years, which may also be high-income years (30–50), it is critically important to ensure that 5 per cent plus of income is 'set aside' annually to provide for the happy and relaxed retirement which everyone is looking forward to.

CHAPTER 4

Finding Your Way Through the Tax Maze

While assessing your financial situation and before determining your investment aims, it is very important to spend some time considering the murky area of tax.

The very word 'tax' conjures up visions of complicated forms, full of obscure figures and words, and also represents a lot of time and effort that needs to be spent when most of us would dearly wish to be doing something else, something less taxing (!) and more interesting.

For most people the objectives are the same:

- we want to arrange our affairs so as to be liable for as little tax as possible;

- we want to pay no more tax than we should;

- we want it all to be as painless, simple and quick as possible;

- we don't want any trip-ups.

The tax implications of your savings and investments are, however, of critical importance and you forget them at your peril.

To find your way through the tax maze in relation to your savings and investments, you must first recognise two key facts.

- To *evade* tax is illegal!

- To *avoid* tax is allowable in certain agreed circumstances.

It is essential to keep on the right side of the law in relation to your tax affairs!

It is important to recognise the different forms of personal tax involved. These are, principally, basic rate income tax, higher rate tax, capital gains tax and inheritance tax. It is important to know exactly where you stand in relation to each and every form of these taxes. This is particularly important when reviewing your possible options, as the tax factor is a vital one to take into consideration.

Income tax

For practical purposes, all your income (other than personal allowances) from whatever source, is subject to British income tax if you are a UK resident. Levels of tax differ in relation to your circumstances, whether or not you are working, etc., and you could find you are eligible for exemptions, allowances and reliefs which come in many forms.

Income from investments

There is, of course, a difference between income which is not taxed at source and that which is in any case wholly tax-free. You do not need to enter tax-free income (such as that earned on your National Savings certificates) on your tax return. You must, however, enter all other income, even though part of it may be tax-free. Examples of categories of income not taxed at source include interest on British Government stocks on the Register of the Department of National Savings, interest on loans to your friends, untaxed income from investments abroad and more recently new investment products such as TESSAs and PEPs (see pages 134, 162).

Tax credits

When a company in which you invest pays you a dividend it also pays the Inland Revenue an amount of tax. This tax is deducted from the money paid to you and is shown as a tax credit on the voucher you receive. It will be taken into account in the overall calculation of your tax liabilities or any repayments due to you. Other investments, such as unit trusts, operate similarly.

In another context, if you have savings in a bank or building society, interest paid to you will be paid after basic rate tax has been deducted. If you are a non tax-payer you will be able to claim this back. If, on the other hand, you are a higher rate tax-payer you will be asked to pay the difference – to the higher rate of tax applicable in your case.

Capital gains tax

If you sell all or part of an asset, any gain you make may be subject to capital gains tax. Whether this is done by sale, gift or exchange, it does constitute a disposal for capital gains purposes. There is an annual allowance and, of course, some statutory exemptions, the most important of which is if there is a transfer between husband and wife.

It is important to know which assets are exempt from capital gains tax. The list is long, but it is especially important to recognise the following:

- your home (or principal residence if you own more than one property);

- a home which you have provided for a dependent relative who is living rent-free (but take care as there is an exact definition of 'dependant');

- some National Savings;

- gambling gains (the money you win at the races, for example);

- a motor car (because most people lose money when selling cars and losses can be offset against gains, so it is not in the Inland Revenue's interest to put capital gains tax on cars).

Inheritance tax

Broadly speaking, inheritance tax is a tax on the value of what you leave when you die. It can include, also, some gifts you make during your lifetime (if you die within seven years of making them). It relates to what happens after you die, and so doesn't really affect your savings and investments except in the sense that you want to look after your near and dear ones after you have gone! Some gifts are tax free (for example a reasonable amount needed to support a dependent relative). Others include maintenance payments to ex-husbands or wives, gifts for education and maintenance for your children if they are still in full-time education and, of course, your annual exemptions. If you don't use the full amount of your exemptions in a specific year you can carry it over to give you a gift fund of double your exemptions for the second year, but you have to use the current year's exemption first.

Who pays inheritance tax depends on the type of gift, but in general terms inheritance tax has to be paid by the donor or giver, and so comes out of his or her estate.

Currently (tax year 1993/4, unchanged for 1994/5) the starting point for inheritance tax stands at total assets less liabilities, resulting in a sum greater than £150,000. After this, tax is payable at 40 per cent.

When considering inheritance tax, it is as well to bear in mind that this represents an attractive area of opportunity for those in the financial services market. As a result you could well be exposed to invitations to attend 'Inheritance Tax Planning' seminars; and other promotional and marketing devices are also used, including incentive gifts, and attractive and very persuasive mailings. If you are in the frame for inheritance tax, do keep in the forefront of your mind the need to retain some flexibility and control over your money in order to be able to meet any costs which may be involved in terms of your own care when you are no longer able to look after yourself. This type of care is very expensive – some two years of terminal 'caring' could easily cost in excess of £100,000 in the not too distant future. So, if you are worried about these matters, resist any attempts the financial services industry may present to you which could end up in your being 'painted into a corner' and not in control of your money when you may need it most to help to buy you some privacy and dignity in old age.

It is especially important to note the rules which apply to inheritance tax as it affects life assurance. Regular premium life policies are a good way to provide help for your relatives and other dependants, as they provide a way of giving away tax-free capital. The premiums themselves count as gifts, but you shouldn't normally need to pay any inheritance tax on them as they will probably fall into one of the tax-free categories.

Inheritance tax tips

• Try to ensure that proceeds of your insurance policies don't count as 'within your estate'. If they do it is likely that they will incur inheritance tax.

• Get the policies concerned, that benefit others, written 'in trust' and then the proceeds can go to the person you have specified.

• Ask your adviser or the insurance company concerned to give you specific and clear guidance – in writing – on any points you want to raise in relation to inheritance tax planning.

The types of policy which are effected in relation to inheritance tax planning include the following.

• **Endowment policies**, which pay out a lump sum on a fixed date, or when you die, if this is earlier. These can be used to give away tax-free capital in your lifetime.

• **Whole life insurance**, paying out only on your death. These can be useful to provide the means of paying any inheritance tax on your estate when you die. In particular they can be valuable to the last survivor of a married couple who have taken out 'cross-over' wills. It pays out on the second death (when the inheritance tax is assessed). These policies are generally at a lower cost than for a policy taken out on a single life.

• **Term insurance**, paying out only if you die before the policy ends. This can be useful if you know that you are likely to leave a large inheritance tax bill for someone else to pay!

In Part 3 you will find more information about all these options.

Claims and allowances

There are many different categories for reliefs, exemptions and allowances in relation to you and your tax. Suffice to say that it pays to find out where you stand. It is known that one in four income tax-payers could be getting a bill which is wrong and that literally thousands of us are paying too much tax!

Tax and the married woman

Independent taxation was introduced from 6 April 1990. From this date:

- married women are responsible for completing their own income tax returns and are separately assessed for tax purposes;

- the husband is no longer responsible for his wife's income and the wife is entitled to privacy in this matter;

- all persons, whether married or single, male or female, will have personal allowances which may be set against their individual income from whatever source;

- in addition, however, a married couple are entitled to a married couple's allowance which they can allocate to either or share;

- personal allowances apply to tax-payers aged 65 to 74, with yet higher allowances for those aged 75 or over.

Maintenance or alimony

Under the simplified rules, ex-spouses who receive maintenance pay no tax on it at all. And the person who pays the maintenance receives tax relief on the payment through receiving some or all of an allowance called the 'maintenance deduction'.

For married women, too, the implications of tax effectiveness are very important. Tax relief angles need to be carefully explored. In Chapter 11, 'Keeping track of your money', the angle of tax effectiveness in relation to selling investments is explored.

Other tax liabilities

It is as well to remember tax liability incurred through benefits in kind, if you have a job and are in receipt of these. They can include medical insurance, 'soft' loans such as season ticket financing and the like. You will need to ensure you budget for these so that you don't get an unpleasant and unwelcome tax demand long after you have spent the money you should have been putting into your sock against future payment to the Revenue! A good idea is to look at the P11D form (the form you may have to fill in which enables the Inland Revenue to assess any benefits in kind which you receive, from private medical insurance to company cars etc.) which every employee has to complete annually. The Revenue sends its large bills in arrears and gives you 30 days to pay so it is wise to be prepared!

Tax and the self-employed

There are many tax disadvantages for the self-employed, but there are many advantages too. For example, if you are employed you will be on the PAYE (pay as you earn) system. As a self-employed person you will not pay tax on this system, but on the profits you make annually, under a Schedule D tax assessment. Here are the advantages of this system.

- More expenses can be claimed and they are generally easier to claim.

- You will get loss relief when you don't make a profit and have to stand a loss, and this can be set against other taxable income.

- If you are in the early years of being self-employed you can carry the losses back against your total income for the previous three years.

- Your home – if you use it for business purposes – becomes a second place of business so that you can claim against your profits a proportion of the expenses such as heating, lighting etc. However, bear in mind that 100 per cent use of a room or rooms in your home for business purposes could present you with capital gains tax difficulties when you sell. Get professional advice before you start, to be safe.

Against this, a major disadvantage is that you have to allow for the complexity of annual accounting etc. And, in the context of the self-employed, value added tax rears its complicated head! Currently this stands at 17.5 per cent on specified goods and services, and we all pay it. If, however, you are in business and have registered for VAT (if your turnover exceeds a certain threshold), you can reclaim the tax you have paid against your business expenditures. As a rough rule of thumb you should be able to get some 20 per cent plus of the tax back, but you will have to spend time making out regular VAT returns and undergo periodic VAT inspection visits, which many people find a gruelling experience.

Tax and children

Each child is an individual tax-payer and entitled to his or her own personal allowance. You will not be taxed on your child's casual earnings or on income arising from gifts made to your children by indulgent relatives. However, if *you* give cash or any other property to your children, income over £100 a year (1993 figures) arising from such gifts will be treated as income to you for tax purposes and you will have to pay the tax due until the child is 18.

If you want to give large sums to your children you can set up an 'irrecoverable trust'. An 'irrecoverable trust' means that you cannot cancel out the transaction in any way and, therefore, you cannot get your money back. The trust can accumulate income until the child is 18 – and you don't have to pay tax on it. Also, a relative can set up a trust which can then pay out income for your child's education and maintenance.

For more information about tax and children the essential first port of call is your local tax office.

CHAPTER 5

Understanding Investments

In order to begin a detailed consideration of what you need to do in relation to your own savings and investments, it is crucial to understand the nature of an investment.

The two elements of investments–growth and income

It is important to recognise that there are two basic elements to each and every investment. These are the capital you invest and the income it produces, and which you can spend or call capital and then invest it, too. At one end of the scale the money you invest, the capital, remains constant and the income earned on it varies (for example, the money you deposit in the bank earns you interest, also the money you invest in your building society). At the other end of the scale, there are investments where the capital grows, but may produce lower income.

Then there are non income-producing investments, such as the money you invest in a work of art. These produce you no income as such, but their capital value may sometimes appreciate impressively over time – often a long time. Alternatively, of course, you may be unlucky and make the unpleasant discovery that their value can depreciate greatly!

Between the two extremes there are, of course, literally hundreds of variations. What is important is to know – or to decide – on the correct 'mix' between income and growth for your particular circumstances. You will find the different popular options in savings and investment described in detail in Part 3 of this book, under three headings: those which offer the most security for your money; those which offer you an each-way bet – some security, some growth; and those which offer you risk of loss, but the expectation of a greater reward if you are lucky.

Before turning straight to Part 3 and selecting your options, however, it is important to understand the system and how it works. Then you need to give thoughtful consideration to developing your investment strategy. This is explained in Chapter 6. After you have thought your way through your investment strategy and decided your priorities in relation to your money, then you are really on the right path to make the most of your financial resources. It is then very likely that you will feel you need to get financial advice. Part 2 of this book will help you select a financial adviser.

Inflation – its relevance and importance

Inflation is really the third element (after growth and income) in evaluating your savings and investment. You need to ensure that your money has a good chance of appreciating – to exceed inflation – and so, hopefully, to offer you the surplus as the real return. In other words you must have a 'hedge' against inflation.

The rate of inflation has risen and fallen rather like a roller-coaster over past years. It is rarely constant and we have seen swings from some 22 per cent annually down to less than 4 per cent annually over the last twenty years. In early 1994 inflation was under 2 per cent. For more information on how inflation can erode your money see Chapter 6.

The time factor

There is a further dimension which you will need to take into consideration, and this is the time factor. You will probably need to look at short, medium and long-term objectives. Think of what you consider these terms to mean. Short term could be say, one year; medium term, say, five years; and long term something in the region of twenty years. But you may wish to relate the phases to different periods of time to suit your particular circumstances. In looking at these, remember that the swings and roundabouts in the financial markets mean there are significant fluctuations over relatively short periods and that, therefore, there may be many of these fluctuations within the period of your long-term planning perspective.

You may be attracted to investing overseas, particularly as there are no current restrictions in investing overseas if you are a UK citizen. In this case foreign exchange rates form a further element in the evaluation of investments. There can be many pitfalls – greater levels of risk to income, an absence of regulation (for example dealing with an unauthorised firm which would mean that you are not protected by the provisions of the financial services regulation), withholding taxes and less security of the asset itself.

General principles in relation to investment policies

Before you can set your investment aims, you need to know a couple of general principles in relation to investment policies.

Diversification

The first principle to consider is whether or not you need to ensure diversification in your savings and investments, and if so to what extent. It is important not to put all your eggs in one basket, but there can be exceptions to this general rule. For example, you may have a share in a business which is your major asset and which it isn't possible or desirable to turn into another form of asset. In general terms, however, it is wise to ensure some degree of diversification in terms of your savings and investments so that you are not in a position of being held hostage to fortune as a result of a future happening which no one is able to predict.

Balance

Here again, it is important for you to ensure that you have a balanced portfolio of savings and investments, and that the balance is in tune with your specific priorities. Part of your resources should be in secure options, for example, building society or bank deposits, and property (e.g. your home). In addition, you should look for some capital appreciation, so part of your resources should be invested in equities, either direct or indirect, through 'starter kit' options (these are the 'collective' investments, such as unit and investment trusts, where you are assured of the professional management of your money in the selection of the stocks and shares in which the funds are invested). They should provide you with some hedge against inflation, as described above. The exact balance between the two options is a matter for you to determine, in line with your particular circumstances.

Setting out your investment aims

When setting out your investment aims, here are the basics you will need to consider.

- **What is the extent of your resources that are available for savings and investment, having provided for 'rainy day' money?** In this context it is important for you to have completed your Wealth Check on page 21, so that you know how much you have. Now you must consider whether you have made adequate provision for your rainy day money which you can get at rapidly if you need it. The ideal amount would be about a year's salary.

- **Is your need for income now?** And in this context it is important to remember the implications of inflation. In any event it is prudent to recognise that you will need to try to attain increasing income. To achieve this you will need to take some level of risk with some of your lump sum money. See the options laid out in Part 3 to make your choice.

- **How long can you afford to 'lock' your money away?** And if you need this to help to provide income at a later stage in your life you can't afford to take many risks with it! You could consider several of the options laid out in Part 3, particularly National Savings index-linked savings certificates, because they protect you from the unpleasant aspects of rising inflation which may be experienced. Index-linked gilts (Government Stocks) are also an attractive option in this context.

- **Do you want your return to be in terms of income or capital growth, or a mixture of the two – and to what extent?** This is very much a matter which only you can determine, but it is very important, in any event, not to put all your eggs into one basket – the abiding rule in prudent savings and investment. In considering this issue you should remember that, with shares, when business is solid, it is the better income earners who have the higher prices owing to market forces. After all, in many cases capital has had to begin as income.

- **Do you need to provide for others after your lifetime?** And, if it is important for you to provide for your heirs, then it is likely that you will be prepared to take more risks with your investments. It is particularly important, in this context, to review your requirements in relation to inheritance tax planning. See pages 30-2.

- **Do you need to prepare for your own future, in terms of redundancy, retirement etc.?** If you do it is very likely that you will have to consider cashing in some of your savings and investments to add income. Certain of the options (see Part 3) make this easier, for example, if you have opted for single premium bonds then you can cash in some of them each year to give you income. Remember, though, that if you have used unit trust options, with a withdrawal scheme, then because the value of the underlying investments goes up and down in tune with the equity markets, you may use a higher proportion of your fund to give you the same income when the price of the units is low. Alternatively, you may have to be content with receiving a lower income at these times. Other investments (such as shares) do not offer you the facility of special withdrawal schemes and you may find that you get a lower price at the time you have to sell the investments to give you the necessary income you need. (In Parts 2 and 3 of this book you will get guidance on how to proceed, in terms of getting financial advice and also in terms of identifying the most popular options for your money.)

- **What are your targets for achievement over five, ten and twenty years?** To be a really effective money manager you need to set these out in as much detail as possible. You will find guidance on how to set about it in Chapter 6 which addresses the subject of how to develop the right investment strategy for you. And, as discussed in Part 2 of this book, how to set about finding investment advice which suits your purpose is another high priority in terms of making the most of your money.

Developing Your Investment Strategy

Having thought about your investment aims in previous chapters, you now need to develop these into a financial plan. How do you set about making such a plan and what should go into it? There are principles to be observed and details to be understood.

Before you start planning in detail, it is a good idea to go back and recap on the important aspects of financial planning which you should already have looked at. Use the following checklist.

Priority recap checklist

1. Is protecting your current home, friends and lifestyle more important to you than protecting your job if this means having to move to a new area?

2. What is your attitude to risk? Are you averse to risk, can you take reasonable amounts of risk, do you have a fundamental need for security, are you unable to cope with change?

3. Are you the sort of person who thrives on challenge? Do you seek out opportunities, want to live life to the full, suffer the 'lows' in order to enjoy the 'highs' which life can provide for those in the fast lane?

4. What would happen if you died prematurely? Check the position with regard to your mortgage – do you have a

suitable insurance policy to ensure that it will be paid off? If you are a woman, would your husband have enough money to hire help to cope with the children? If you are a man would your wife have enough to live on or would she have to get a job? Have you thought about term assurance? (see Part 3, page 170).

5. Have you made a will? Are you aware of the problems that can arise from intestacy?

6. Have you got enough 'rainy day' money to cope with any unexpected emergency?

7. Have you already got a stake in the future? For example, are you planning for retirement through pension provision? Do you intend to start a little business or to begin a new hobby?

Finally, it is useful to know that you will start a new year at least no worse off than you started the current year. This is sometimes not as easy as it sounds, but it is a useful discipline to set yourself. For example, say you started out last year with a realisation that you had not put sufficient money away in your rainy day fund and also in your nest egg. So you increased your savings by taking out a regular savings plan using a unit trust as a vehicle and made provision for another £15 a month to be held in your savings account at the bank. Now this year, you have recognised that you need to do more and are uncertain as to which options you should consider first. By referring to Part 3 of this book you should find the answers to your questions.

Now you are in a position to plan ahead, and to determine your own priorities for your money, and your resources generally.

Drawing up your financial plan

How do you set about making a financial plan and what goes into it?

First, you need to decide to sit down and do it. Take a clean piece of paper, a pen or pencil, and get your head down. It probably won't take more than half an hour and it could easily turn out to be the best investment of your time you ever make!

Now you need to decide what to put on your piece of paper. Here is a step-by-step guide.

Step 1

Decide the time-frame of your financial plan. For example, choose to put down one year from now (covering the short term), five years from now (for the medium term), ten years from now (for the longer medium term) and even perhaps twenty years from now (over the long term). What are your short, medium and long-term requirements?

Step 2

Decide where you wish to be under all the time-frames you have set out. Make this simple and practical. Here is an example.

FINANCIAL PLAN

In **one year's time** I want to have reduced my ongoing debts, by identifying targets and also increasing my savings and investments by a realistic target.

In **five years' time** I wish to have eradicated all outstanding debts, and also tried to increase my savings and investments by 75 per cent, also to be sure that I am keeping carefully in mind what options are tax effective and inflation proof in my case.

In **ten years' time** I want to have moved to a better and bigger home, made real progress in terms of planning for my retirement, increased my savings and investment portfolio to an extent that offers appreciation by inflation with a sizeable extra 'comfort' margin.

For the long term, over say **twenty years**, I want to know that I have secured a comfortable retirement, that I will then be enjoying a lifestyle which satisfies me, that I am preparing a tax-effective disposition of assets in terms of securing a satisfactory inheritance tax position for my family.

Step 3

Use the information you gathered in the priority recap checklist. Now you must decide your priorities. This means looking carefully at what means happiness and quality of life for you. You will need to be realistic, deciding what type of lifestyle you want or need, whether material wealth is an important factor, whether health is likely to be a future issue, and, of course, the level of risk you are happy with in terms of decisions you will need to make on savings and investments. In this context, too, you will need to decide whether you need to invest for income or for growth.

Step 4

It is time, now, to look at whose help you will need to ensure you have the best chances of implementing your financial plan. This means being very clear as to whether you intend to do the majority of the work and the planning yourself, or whether you need the help of a financial adviser for this purpose – one of the range of specialist advisers, brokers, dealers or other experts around in the financial market-place. In all probability you will decide to opt for expert guidance and in Part 2 of this book you will find all the information you need on seeking financial advice. There are many vital things to consider: whether you will be happiest dealing with an independent financial adviser, aiming to choose the best options for you from the entire range on the market; or a tied adviser with the back-up of a large organisation but able to offer only the products or services of the company under whose auspices the adviser is authorised. A further important factor is to ensure that he or she is properly authorised, and to know whether he or she is really committing their principals, or merely an unbacked entrepreneur. You can do this by phoning the Securities and Investments Board (see page 121) to check the status of the organisation you are thinking of dealing with.

Step 5

Having written down your financial plan, it is most important to review it regularly. You should do this at least quarterly. In this way, if things are going wrong, or you are in danger of having your financial ship blown off course, you will be in a position to rectify matters sooner rather than later. There are steps you should take to review your plan. These are outlined on page 108 of this book. Keeping track of your money – and your adviser – is the subject matter of Chapter 11 of this book.

Your strategy for savings and investment

Having determined your priorities, and the type of advice you need, the degree to which you feel confident of your own knowledge of the financial services industry and how it works, and the degree to which you feel you need the help of a specialist, it is now time to set out your strategy on savings and investment. This will depend very much on your current position with regard to your age, your health, your family and work situation (which in turn affects your tax position), and any windfalls you may be expecting, as a result perhaps of maturing insurance policies or well-wishing relatives.

It is likely that you will start with a proportion of low-risk investments, e.g. deposits in banks, building societies and perhaps National Savings investment, then, if funds allow it, adding some medium-risk equity investments, e.g. unit trusts or investment trusts. Finally, if you are prepared to accept risk, you should consider putting a small proportion of your overall funds in higher risk investments, in the hope of getting a higher level of reward, perhaps direct investment in shares. Remember also that these last options, the higher risk investments, should be considered as long-term investments, and that some people love to feel the excitement of 'playing with money', such as gambling in a casino or 'being an angel' (investing in theatrical productions).

How inflation can erode your money

Another matter to be considered carefully before you set your strategy is the effect of inflation on your savings and investment. There are some options which you may be considering where the value of your capital stays the same, not allowing for the effects of inflation. To keep the sums simple, even though at the time of writing inflation is low, say under 4 per cent, let us look at a position if inflation was running at a higher rate, say 10 per cent (which was the position not so long ago and could be again). If this is the case, if you invest £1,000 now on a non equity basis, and spend any income you get from the investment, then want to get back your cash in, say, five years' time, your £1,000 will only be worth £621 if the inflation rate stayed constant at 10 per cent a year over those five years. And, since most investments are long term, say over twenty years, that £1,000 would be worth only £149 on the basis of the same scenario over that length of time.

Remember, though, that you cannot have your cake and eat it!

The effect of inflation on your financial resources can be quite devastating if you have not prepared for it. This, therefore, is a matter of priority to take carefully into consideration when setting your strategy with regard to savings and investment. The figures below should make the point more clearly:

What £1,000 today will be worth over 5, 10, 15 and 20 years:

	5	10	15	20
At 10% inflation	£621	£386	£239	£149
At 5% inflation	£784	£614	£481	£377

There are, of course, some options on saving and investment which protect you from the effects of inflation and will be discussed in Part 3.

More about risk

You should already be aware of your attitude to risk as the matter has been raised before in this book. It is vital to successful financial planning. You should give deep consideration to your attitude to risk before deciding your strategy for savings and investment. You will either be able to take risks or you will be averse to risk.

If you dislike risk, are frightened by it, this is nothing to be ashamed of. Just recognise the fact and don't allow others to persuade you that options are 'safe' when you believe there could be an element of risk which could worry you in the future. It's your money after all.

In addition to your attitude to risk, however, there is the fact that there are two major additional risks you could face with regard to your investments. These are as follows.

Risk to your capital

The lump sum you may have invested could well be at risk. Sometimes this is at low levels, and sometimes the levels of risk are high. They are generally related to the return which is promised when you buy. Do remember very clearly that a promise is not a guarantee and that the word 'guarantee' itself is used far too frequently in talking about financial services. By far the wisest course is to be very cynical about promises or guarantees, and then the surprises you receive can be pleasant and not unpleasant!

The risk to your capital is again determined by many factors, from the effectiveness of management to the availability of markets and demands, and the economic conditions prevailing in the UK and internationally. Investments can include your unit trusts, shares, and even the antique furniture and bits of family jewellery you own. These latter are more frequently identified as 'alternative investments'. If you do want to realise your money from them you may be in for a sharp shock as the return you get can be less than half of the insurance valuation and if you do find out the mark-up levels you have to pay to your dealer who handles the task for you, you may have to reach for the smelling salts!

Risk to your income

Naturally enough the extent of your return from your investment in terms of income paid to you will vary, depending on the nature of the investment and its performance. The performance can vary because of management effectiveness, national and international economic changes, and a host of other variables. The worst scenario is that you might not get any income at all ... so be prepared.

Don't put all your eggs in one basket

As we have seen, the wisest course in terms of deciding on your investment strategy is not to put all your eggs in one basket. Choose to spread your money around. Decide first of all how much of your money you can afford to put at risk in order to get that higher return. Remember, however, that it is not usually economic to buy shares in amounts of less than £2,000 per bite. As a rule of thumb, from which you can start to tailor your own investment strategy, take a look at this example, for a pretty average sort of person:

- One-third of your overall assets should be in property – in owning your own home and the like. Even though the property market has been unbelievably erratic over recent years, if you own your house you do have land, bricks and mortar to show for your money – and a home. Equally it is important not to be in 'over your head', so ensure that you are pragmatic and realistic in terms of what the property is worth, and the proportion of your income you need to spend on mortgage payments, home maintenance and the like. Ideally this should be not more than 30 per cent.

- One-third at least should be in safety-first options, that you can turn into cash quickly and easily. In this context you will find National Savings, bank and building society and some insurance options, TESSAs and the like (see Part 3 for more information).

- Then, depending on the level of risk with which you are comfortable, you are ready to put up to one-third of your financial resources into investment products such as unit and investment trusts, shares etc., which should offer you a better return for the greater level of risk you are being asked to take. But remember, too, that they may go down in value and that is the risk you take!

In Part 3 you will find an explanation of the different types of savings and investments, together with an indication of the upside and the downside of each, together with a risk rating indication.

Investment for income or growth, for now or later?

It is now time to look at *why* you are investing, at your objective, at what it is all for ... Are you investing for income or for growth, or perhaps a mix of the two? You need to know where you stand on this point. The next decision is to face up to whether you are wanting income now, or later ... (Growth is necessarily a long-term issue.)

Why you want the income needs to be identified. Is it for you? For now? Or later? Or for others after your death? It is always important to know why the income is needed.

You need to be clear about when you may want to cash in the investment, too. You may be investing so that you can buy something – for example a share in a business of your own. You may be investing on a rolling basis, so that the money is there when you need it in, say, ten years' time. You may be investing to increase the size of a nest egg which want to be sure you have, or to cope with, perhaps, a critical illness which you know you may some day have to face.

So, to help you, fill in this simple form with the aid of your financial plan, as set out on pages 43-6.

BASIC INVESTMENT STRATEGY

Short term (one to five years) Define your aim in, say a hundred words.

Example: I believe that I have a realistic expectation that my income will be rising strongly over this period, and that, therefore, I can afford to erode my nest egg to a small extent in order to take in a special holiday for all the family, since it is likely that next year the children will want to take holidays on their own. My aim is to add to the quality of family life by taking the family on a holiday of a lifetime and to replenish my nest egg as soon as possible.

Long term (five to twenty years) Define your objective in, say a hundred words.

Example: My income is likely to fall between the fifteen to twenty-year term. I need to be sure that I have built up my savings to the necessary extent to allow for this, so I aim to research the extent to which I can add regular savings to my nest egg and to confirm that nest egg money is safe and that there are not better options available. (Part 3 should help in this context.)

My attitude to risk is:
aversion?
excitement?
apprehension but interest?

While you are setting your strategy, always keep two priorities well in mind. We have already looked at these, but it is worth reviewing them again.

The first is the need to review your investments regularly. The whole nature of the new global investment market is that it moves rapidly. You need to know how your money is moving within the system. You should check up, formally, by spending an hour or so on this matter at least once a quarter, preferably monthly or even more frequently than that. These matters are dealt with in detail in Chapter 11.

The second is to be acutely aware of the current level of interest rates. Ideally you are looking to ensure that your investment return includes a hedge against the rate of inflation and then some, at the very least. (Even if this means that you are expecting too much at least it gives you a target to shoot for!) If you are involved in a major growth strategy it is possible that you may be prepared to take initial losses before the strong capital growth can be discernible. Be careful, though, to find out what the true rates of interest which you are getting from your money are, and the risks and their extent. It is as well to recognise that interest rates can be rather less than they seem! A high interest rate delivered infrequently (say annually) can be, effectively, a lower level of return than a more modest interest rate delivered more frequently (say monthly)! These differences can make all the difference to the rate of return you receive over the years ... Work it out, month by month, for the year and see.

To find out the 'true' rate of return you get, ensure you are comparing like with like. For example, rates of interest quoted on National Savings certificates are annual, a true rate of return. The interest you receive from your building society or local authority loan (see Part 3) may be added more often, say twice a year. So to compare them you will need to ask the building society or local authority what their rate is over a year, in order to contrast with the return on your National Savings certificates.

Also, today, it is very likely that you will be paid interest on most types of savings (for example on your bank or building society deposit accounts) net of basic rate tax – this means that you won't have to pay any more tax on the savings if you are a basic rate tax-payer. If you are a non tax-payer you can arrange to have payment made without the deduction of tax. If you are a higher rate tax-payer, you will need to stump up the difference between the basic rate and the higher rate of tax.

The abiding rule, in terms of your investments, is to compare like with like on interest rates, on tax, on everything possible – *before* you make your final choices on investments and to check up on them regularly.

Your personal financial planning chart

If you enlist help from a financial adviser he or she is required to complete a Fact Find to determine your circumstances. Here is an example of the type of information he or she will be trying to establish and it will be helpful for you to fill it in for yourself. While this may look in some ways similar to the Wealth Check which is featured on page 21 of this book, it is in truth a different animal. The Fact Find incorporates many features which are determined by the Financial Services Act. What is important is to relate this information to your own Wealth Check and your financial planning chart, using the step-by-step approach shown earlier (pages 44-6).

What your financial adviser will want to know

The main aim of your financial adviser will be to:

● establish the use that you are currently making of your financial assets;

● define your needs as you perceive them, after discussion, to discover what they really are;

● determine the gap that exists between what you have and what you want;

● determine, in consultation with you, how best to fill that gap.

In trying to arrive at the above, your financial adviser will be aware that clients do not always accurately assess their financial requirements, also that clients sometimes object to questioning which they may find too intrusive, no matter how well intentioned.

The checklist below gives you a basis for understanding the type and nature of information your adviser will want to build about you and your current position.

FINANCIAL CHECKLIST

1. Personal details

This includes date of your birth, your general state of health, whether or not you smoke and the level of your alcohol intake. All these will affect any insurance premium levels. Where you live, your job, its industry and your position within it (if you are employed), how long you have held it, will all be relevant information.

2. Family details

Your adviser will need to know what dependants you have, whether family or not, and the nature of your responsibilities to them.

3. Income

Naturally your adviser will need comprehensive information about your current income, earned and/or unearned.

4. Property

All property you own, with its overall value, is vital information needed by your adviser – as well as any mortgages or loans against these.

5. Other assets

Information on investments, insurance policies and any other assets will be needed.

6. Financial interests

Your adviser will need to know your likes and dislikes in relation to financial products and services, whether you want to improve your current lifestyle, save for a holiday or school fees; your plans for the short, medium and long term. He or she will also need to have information on any liabilities and these will need to be quantified.

7. Tax position

Your adviser will want to know your tax status, whether or not you need to plan to be more tax effective in future.

8. Inheritance position

Your adviser will need to know what your plans are in this regard, and whether or not you want to plan to mitigate the possible level of inheritance tax to be paid. He or she will also need to know if you expect to benefit from an inheritance and when this is likely to be.

9. Current arrangements

The present position with regard to pensions, permanent health arrangements, sickness and accident insurance cover needs to be known.

10. Risk

Your adviser needs to know your attitude to risk, also whether you want to avoid it at all costs. He or she will seek to establish your general willingness to accept risk, and the risk mix in percentage terms related to the type of savings and investment options you are prepared to consider.

11. Past experience

It will be helpful to your adviser if you filled in any background on past experiences with other financial advisers and the reason for making the change to him or her.

CHAPTER 7

Special Situations

Throughout your life, you will be faced with many different situations. It is sometimes difficult to see the logical way forward when you find yourself in one of these 'special situations'. Some typical special situations are outlined here. For the answers to be as accurate as possible, the views of experts in the regulation of financial services have been sought in the compilation of the answers to the questions.

What to do if you want to find out about your pension

Bill is forty-five and has worked for the same company for fifteen years, during which he has contributed to a final salary pension scheme. He is now nervous about possible future redundancy and wants to check up on his pension rights and provisions, as well as what he may get in terms of the State pension. Above all, he wants to know if his pension is 'safe'. How should he set about finding out?

The answer is given by Barry Woolley, a former president of the Life Insurance Association and a council member of the Financial Intermediaries, Managers and Brokers Regulatory Association (FIMBRA). His firm is Charter Financial Planning Limited of Preston.

I would suggest that Bill write to the trustees/administrators of the pension scheme for confirmation of his benefit entitlement on redundancy. At the same time he should seek confirmation as to whether or not the scheme is 'contracted in or out' of SERPS.

The Social Security Act 1985 disclosure requirements detail that the trustees must provide, among other things, on request:

- benefit statement;
- transfer value estimates;
- latest actuarial valuation;
- latest scheme report including audited accounts.

If he requires personal financial advice, he should contact an independent financial adviser (IFA), who should be engaged on a fee basis to confirm what the benefits are likely to be worth, what options are available under the scheme and the suitability of a transfer on early leaving. In order to identify a suitable IFA, contact should be made with either IFAP (see page 175) or SIB (see page 172) for SIB registered IFAs.

If he does not require personal financial advice, but requires advice only in relation to his specific options and queries in relation to the scheme, he can contact the Occupational Pensions Advisory Service, either directly or through the Citizen's Advice Bureau. He can get both telephone numbers from the phone book or by calling BT.

As regards his State scheme benefits, for general queries there are various Department of Social Security leaflets available, for example:

- FB6 – *Retiring?*
- N1196 – *Social Security Benefit Rates*
- N1230 – *Unemployment Benefit and Your Occupational Pension*
- NP46 – *Retirement Pensions.*

It is probably too early to obtain any exact figures from the DSS, but it should be stressed that a good independent financial adviser could give him an indication of his entitlement.

For further information see Chapter 9 of this book.

What to do if you think you may need to transfer your pension

John has a senior appointment with a nationally known organisation. He has ten years' rights in a particular pension scheme and has been advised by his bank to transfer out of this to a section 32 Buy-out. The bank has recommended another scheme to him, but as yet he has taken no action. Previously he had twelve months in another pension scheme belonging to his then employers. Moving to his present employers he responded to advice to join his present pension scheme, investing his DSS contributions in this. He now needs advice as to what he should look for in relation to making the right decision. He is forty, married, with two children aged twelve and six. How should he set about it?

The answer to this question comes from Gareth Marr, deputy chairman of FIMBRA. His company is Moores Marr Bradley Ltd of Central Milton Keynes.

John should first consider his future career plans and aims for retirement. The decision to join the new employer's scheme should normally indicate a medium to long-term commitment to his new role. A clear understanding of the benefits provided under the scheme with particular reference to options on retirement, the way the benefits build up (final salary or money purchase) and the valuable 'death in service' cover for lump sums and spouses' pensions in view of the family commitments, are all important points to review.

The transfer options on his two previous schemes need to be considered in full. It would be unusual for the short, twelve-month service scheme to offer more than a refund of contributions less tax as preservation of accrued benefits only usually applies after two years' service. If a transfer value is available this should be reviewed with the options offered on the ten-year service scheme.

Independent advice is necessary to ensure all the options are considered. Briefly, these are as follows.

- Leave the benefits in the existing schemes. Valuable guarantees could be given up on a transfer, and benefits are now revalued by law at 5 per cent or the present rate of inflation if less – no more frozen pensions!

- Transfer to the new employer's scheme. If a long-term career is planned serious consideration needs to be given to the 'added benefits' the new scheme will offer for the transfer value. If the scheme is a final salary arrangement these could prove valuable, being linked to remuneration at retirement.

- Transfer to a 'section 32' or personal pension policy. The considerations are lengthy and complex, but such a transfer usually involves giving up guaranteed benefits for an expectation of a greater reward at retirement. The differences between the two contracts need to be explained in full.

FIMBRA has produced a useful *Guidance Note No. 7* which details the main consideration to be taken into account in this decision. A FIMBRA-regulated IFA will provide a copy on request or the document can be obtained direct from FIMBRA (address on page 172).

What to do if you want to change from an endowment to a repayment mortgage

Mary is thirty-nine, a single parent with two children (aged eleven and seven) to support. Six years ago she took out a twenty-five year mortgage with a leading building society – using a low-cost endowment. She is now nervous about any possible gap between what the payout will be on the endowment policy and the level of the mortgage repayment she will need to make in due course. She has written to both the building society and the insurance company, and finds their replies impossible to understand and unravel because of regulatory reporting obligations. She simply wants to know what to do to check whether or not she will be better off changing her mortgage to a simple twenty-year repayment mortgage. What should she do?

This answer comes from a senior authority in the 'tied sector'.

The first consideration would be for Mary to seek appropriate advice regarding her situation. Possible ports of call would be:

- **the building society;**
- **the insurance company;**
- **an independent financial adviser.**

Any of the above should be able to assist Mary with unravelling the replies received so that she can understand the current situation.

On approaching the selected adviser, Mary may wish to consider the following issues:

- **her current and future ability to pay her mortgage through her regular income/or possible lump sums;**

- life assurance requirements in respect of her two children;

- any current surrender value of the low-cost endowment and loss that would result from cancellation or surrender;

- whether the selected adviser has a vested interest in either pursuing the existing contract or recommending a further investment;

- any costs involved in rearranging her mortgage;

- past investment returns of the insurance company;

- the relative merits of endowment and repayment mortgages.

What to do if you need to plan for school fees

James and Jean are in their late thirties and have three children, aged two, five and seven. James has a good job and ideally they would like to send the children to private schools. In addition, James and Jean's parents have indicated that they would like to help, but although James and Jean are prepared to accept some modest help, they would prefer to plan to pay for the majority of the school fees themselves. How do they find suitable advice and what options are available to them and to the children's grandparents?

This answer comes from a senior authority in the tied sector.

The first consideration would be to locate a specialist financial adviser who is active in the area of school fees planning. The Independent Schools Advisory Service would be worth contacting in the first instance. The bursar of the school, if one has been selected, may also be able to advise if an advance payment scheme exists.

Factors to be considered are as follows:

- their attitude towards risk and investment management control;
- the ages from which fees would be required for each child and the duration of this requirement;
- the amounts of any fees, in today's terms, assuming fees are required for all three children;
- accessibility required to any capital sums invested;
- regularity and security of income;
- continuation of funding in the event of death or disablement.

What to do if you want to give money to children

Harold and Phyllis have four grandchildren (in their teens) who are very dear to them. They don't want to spoil them, but they would like to give them money, some now to provide some desirable 'extras', such as help towards the cost of a holiday, and some later, when they will be setting up home and starting out on family life. In particular Harold and Phyllis need to be sure that the majority of the money will be safe from enthusiastic, over-indulgent spending sprees! What should they do?

Gareth Marr answers in these terms.

Harold and Phyllis are able to give money to their grandchildren in highly tax-efficient ways.

For smaller sums of money, to provide immediate extras, the grandparents could make gifts directly to the children, perhaps by opening a building society account in the name of each child. The tax advantage to the grandparents is that provided these gifts are within the annual gift exemption of two times £3,000 a year (1993 figures), these amounts would not be included in their estate for inheritance tax purposes, provided that the overall ceiling had not been exceeded. As each child has their own personal allowance, interest in the building society accounts should accumulate without deduction of basic rate tax.

There are broadly two choices for the generation of lump sums for the grandchildren in, say, five to ten years' time.

The first is by direct investments specifically earmarked for individual grandchildren. A particular attractive lump sum investment without risk is the National Savings Children's Bonus Bond which will provide a tax-free lump sum in five years. If the grandparents are willing to enter into an ongoing commitment, then Baby Bonds issued by friendly societies are attractive, as are endowment policies for children, available from a few insurance companies.

The second way is for the grandparents to set up an accumulation and maintenance trust for the benefit of all four grandchildren. These have the advantages of allowing the trustees discretion to provide both income and capital when it is required, an avoidance of the ten-yearly charge to inheritance tax levied on other discretionary trusts, and after seven years the initial gift would be free from any possible inheritance tax on the grandparents' estate. As such a trust needs to be drawn up by a solicitor, it is only really relevant to larger gifts. It is particularly important that the trust is empowered to include 'wider range' investments such as life assurance policies.

By taking careful account of the grandparents' attitude towards risk, a range of tax-efficient investments can be arranged to benefit the four grandchildren.

What to do if you want to make a will

Sheila is a widow in her late sixties. Her husband died some five years ago, leaving her well provided for. Her family is grown up and away from home. She has five grandchildren. Now Sheila is concerned to ensure that her will makes provision for the family, but also recognises some friends who have been of great help to her during her husband's terminal illness, and also makes provision for one or two of their joint 'good causes'. Sheila and her husband had made simple 'cross-over' wills, but she now needs to make another will so that her wishes are properly taken care of. She particularly needs guidance on who should be her executors and how much this will cost. Where does she start and how much will it all cost?

Barry Woolley comments.

In this case Sheila has already had contact with a solicitor when she made the simple 'cross-over' will in conjunction with her husband. We would suggest that she contacts those solicitors who dealt with this on her husband's death as long as she was happy with their service then.

If she is not happy with the previous solicitor then she could approach the Law Society for a recommendation or alternatively she could make contact with a will writer in her locality, identifying these through the *Yellow Pages*. While she could purchase a will-writing kit from a stationer's, this course of action is not recommended as there are pitfalls. Perhaps the best way for her to make contact with a new solicitor is to obtain a recommendation from someone whom she is close to who has used a solicitor on a frequent basis, perhaps someone in business.

While it is possible that a family friend could act as an executor it is recommended that professional services are engaged. Most appropriately the solicitor who draws up her will could provide the services necessary or, indeed, if she felt inclined she could use her bank in these circumstances.

As regards the costs for drawing up a will, these are likely to range for the simplest will from £40 up to more complicated arrangements where the fee would be in the order of £100 (1993 figures). For the services of a professional firm acting as executor then the charge is likely to be in the order of 1 per cent of the value of the estate.

What to do if you face redundancy

Jim is in his late forties. He has been working for the same company for ten years – in the construction industry. Now he fears that it may not be long before he faces redundancy. He is anxious to prepare himself for this so that he and his family are not 'thrown' should the situation arise. He is married, with three children (a boy aged twelve, and two girls of seven and five). Jim wants to know to whom he can talk, what are the questions he should ask and the sums he should do so that he can know where he stands. What advice should he be given?

Again, advice comes from Barry Woolley.

Does Jim have any advisers? If so he should talk to them, since some now specialise in redundancy counselling. Jim should make enquiries with his employers to determine if they provide redundancy counselling services in-house or whether they contract out for services.

If nothing emerges from the above enquiries, then Jim could make contact with his local Citizen's Advice Bureau, in addition to which he should make contact with the following to determine his position:

- his building society/bank about his mortgage arrangements and what facilities they have to protect mortgage payments in the event of redundancy or, alternatively, if none is available, what preparations he should make to avoid any catastrophe;

- he should contact the Department of Social Security to obtain an indication of what benefits are available to him;

- he should enquire of his employer what redundancy payments are likely, but if he feels unsure about approaching his employer for this specific advice, he could perhaps contact ex-colleagues who found themselves in a similar situation;

- can he make additional savings in the meantime in order to help protect his future position and does he have any money already put by and, if so, can he get easy access to it?

- does he have any life assurance policies that have a cash value and that are not tied into other arrangements such as his mortgage? He should make enquiries of the companies involved to determine what values are available.

Does Jim have contact with an independent financial adviser? If so he should approach this individual or, alternatively, if he has no contact, then he could enquire of IFAP to determine the names of such firms in his locality whom he might approach for advice. In making this approach, he should already have calculated his minimum budget required to maintain a reasonable lifestyle, thus identifying any areas of expense that can be either cut out immediately, or later, once his position is confirmed.

Partnership problems

Amy's partner of twelve years died unexpectedly. Previously they had shared everything ... the costs of living, the house (the mortgage was in her name as she had bought the house before she met Tom), the holidays, etc. Amy had been working, but they recently moved home and were starting afresh in the country. Now Amy discovers that, although a will had been written it hadn't been signed, and although divorce proceedings had been started with his wife the papers hadn't been filed. So, she loses out – completely. Her partner's widow inherits all he left, even though some of it, in truth, belongs to Amy. She has talked to solicitors and had the advice of a barrister. Is there any other action she can take? Are the services of a financial adviser relevant in this context?

Gareth Marr answers the questions in these terms.

It is too late to lament about what has happened, but unmarried couples should always pay special attention to their financial affairs. Any joint financial obligations should always be insured. This can be done very cheaply with a term assurance which should, of course, be written in trust for the benefit of the other partner. This would have left Amy with some financial help even if Tom's property had reverted back to his widow.

One area that does need investigation, however, is any lump sum life assurance benefits that Tom may have had while a member of his company's pension scheme. Because these benefits, by necessity, are written under discretionary trust, it should be reasonably easy to persuade the trustees that Amy is entitled to some of this benefit, as she was financially dependent upon Tom at his death.

Amy now needs to look to the future and ensure that her own financial affairs are in the best of order. An independent financial adviser could provide help as to the best way of providing income now if she should need it and, also, pension planning advice for the future. Amy can no longer rely upon Tom's pension in

her retirement. An independent financial adviser could also help to provide the right sort of life cover for Amy to ensure that her dependants never find themselves in the same situation as she has.

PART TWO

GETTING FINANCIAL ADVICE

In Part 1 of this book you found out how to develop your own investment strategy. Throughout the book I stress that knowledge is power, and the degree of your understanding of financial services and products directly affects the results you will be able to achieve from your savings and investments. This part of the book deals with the complex financial market-place. It will explore the system, help you to choose an adviser and guide you on how to make your investments work well for you.

CHAPTER 8

How the System Works

This chapter aims to give you some insights into the complex market-place of the financial services industry.

The financial services industry – who does what

Think of the financial services industry as a giant market-place. Today it is a global industry, operating twenty-four hours a day, seven days a week – as can be seen from the radio and TV news programmes, and our daily newspapers. The market exists to buy and sell money, expressed in terms of shares (or equities) and other 'financial instruments'. Today, too, the power and influence of the individual in this global market-place has shrunk to almost total insignificance, as we can all recognise, some of us to our personal cost!

But it is possible to help make the market-place work for you, rather than against you. And that is what you must try to achieve. Everyone in the financial services industry is being paid his or her salary out of your money and the interest it earns. Of course they have to be paid for the services they provide for you. But you should make sure you know how it all works and avoid bad use of the service. After all, the money managers need your money, so you have to ensure that you let them reward you!

The very first point to recognise is that it is your choice as to whether the financial market-place controls you or you control it. Yes, you can control it by being aware of some of its complexities, and by being aware in much more detail, and with sensitivity, of what you want to achieve with your savings and investments, and the nature and level of the risks you are prepared to take.

The financial market-place

Essentially you should think of money as a commodity and recognise that it has no value in itself. Money is merely a means of exchange, for things, goods, shares in businesses and services (including insurance, investment or pensions, as well as holidays, policing the neighbourhood etc.) that may be important to you, even vital. This means that making the most of your money involves knowing what you are exchanging for what.

The money markets are simply a means of buying and selling money (albeit in different forms) as a form of commodity. The degree of added value (or deficit) provided by the financial institutions is a complex issue. It is an issue hotly debated by those who believe that the reward taken by the money managers from getting their 'turn' or 'slice' off every transaction going through is excessive by comparison with the value provided by those who are involved in the actual wealth-production process, for example manufacturing industry. This is not to decry the value of service industries, of which finance is one, but to help you get some sense of perspective, so that you can make sure you are in control at all times and, while taking the advice which you may be offered, that you can make very sure of its value when making a decision. You should also understand the nature of the vested interest of the person or institution who may be offering you a product or service, as well as the level of the remuneration they may be earning from you!

It's your money after all. You must always remember this. You must aim to be always in the driving seat, getting from the industry what you want for your money and not the other way round. And the individual can really achieve this – if he or she understands the principles involved.

On the personal level, we deal with the money machines of

the world through the money managers. Most of these will be all too familiar to you, but it is as well, for the purposes of this book, to spell out those with whom you will be most in touch.

The money managers

The bank manager

He or she offers you general advice and will be able to get specialist advice, if you want it, from the bank's stockbroker, insurance broker, investment adviser etc. All the clearing banks have now turned themselves into financial supermarkets (or they are in the process of doing so). Some of them resort to sales techniques which may not always be regarded as quite ethical, in order to extend the turnover of their branches through the sale of other products, such as insurance and unit trusts, to you as their existing customer.

In the main there is nothing illegal in this, but do be aware of what is going on. There have been many cases where a bank manager has called in a customer, perhaps to go over some aspect of their bank account, who approaches the interview with some apprehension because, after all, many of us still retain a historic sense of awe of the bank manager. Then, during the interview, it just so happens that the manager of, perhaps, the insurance section of the branch pops in and is introduced to you, the customer. Surprise, surprise – you can end up finding that you have bought some of the insurance products which the bank is selling and these can be the products of just one insurance company – which the bank has agreed to push, when others might well have suited you better!

It is well worth keeping in the front of your mind when you are doing business with a bank that many bank employees are, one way or the other, getting performance-related pay. Some of this is unquestionably related to the extent to which they are able to persuade you to do more business with them. And the performance-related bonus is usually higher if in-house products are sold rather than products available from their related independent financial advisory arms.

It is also important to recognise that all the major clearing banks are 'tied' – they can only advise you to buy their own products and services, or those of just one insurance company with whom they have a contractual arrangement. Therefore, you do not have the benefit of knowing whether or not there are other options, or similar or better products available, which may be more appropriate in your case, and/or could offer you better value for money. The availability of independent – and normally better value – advice is there for the asking, but *you must ask*!

Nevertheless, you should keep in mind, too, that your bank manager does perform a very useful service. Arguably, it is also up to you to ensure that you are getting what you want from the relationship – don't leave it all to him or her – or the bank!

The building society manager

He or she is your local link with the building society. You will generally find a more user-friendly atmosphere within a building society, where the staff are trained to be much more warm and welcoming than you will find in many banks. Don't be fooled by this! Today, the building societies are in the same business as the banks – they are turning themselves, too, into financial supermarkets, and all may not be quite what you think or may expect in relation to their business practices. It is as well to remember, too, at the time of writing, that nearly all the major building societies are operating as 'tied' organisations – unable to offer you a spread of investment products taken from the whole range available. They are limited to selling their own products and those of just one insurance or other company with whom they have a tied relationship. This – as with all banks – seriously inhibits your chances of ensuring that you are getting the best value for your money. The largest building society to offer independent advice is the Bradford & Bingley, followed by the Yorkshire, but most of the major well-known building societies are tied. Why? For the simple reason that it generally pays them very much better – at your expense!

Here again, it is up to you to see that you are getting what you want from your building society manager – and the society itself. The service culture of the building societies is long established, so remind them of it and use it!

The insurance agent

The insurance company is really the giant in terms of your savings and investments. You give them your money regularly, in insurance premiums, pension contributions etc., and, in due course, they pay you out, when the policies mature. Over recent years, however, they have developed their strengths, and have become savings and investment supermarkets of yet another variety. Although they do have some shops on local high streets, mostly they operate through vast direct sales forces of insurance agents who seek you out as a potential customer. Some of these are tied agents and have been less than desirable, and weaknesses in this system of selling have now been acknowledged by the insurance companies who are seeking to address the requirements of the financial regulators as to training, competence and selling standards. Many thousands of people have lost literally hundreds of millions of pounds between them, because unscrupulous agents had sold them products which were not appropriate, and therefore did without that greater growth potential in capital or income that a more suitable investment should have provided.

It is as well to keep in mind, too, that recent events have exposed new and unexpected risks for insurance companies. They have to plan for the cover to be delivered to their customers, and for this to be affordable and paid for in the form of premiums. The risks are many and varied, and some may not have existed or been imagined when policies were started, but the policies then had to cover them, sometimes years later. They can include unusual weather conditions (like the major storms of 1987), industrial disasters, sea coast erosion, unsuspected and unattributable subsidence, dread diseases (such as AIDS and cancer), aeroplane crashes, hurricanes, turbulent money markets (Black Monday, October 1987), terrorism (such as IRA bombings in London) etc. All have eroded some of the historic financial strengths of insurance companies. These factors, as well as the indifferent management standards in parts of the industry, have led one distinguished American insurance tycoon to conclude that many of the most important US insurance companies have lost 50 to 60 per cent of their value in the seven years to 1993. In turn, this may well mean that returns in terms of bonuses may be lower in the years to come than they have been in the past.

Having said all that, your insurance agent can be very useful to you and, in the main, the company he or she serves recognises that good business means satisfying a lot of customers over long periods of time. Recognise that your responsibility is to ensure you make the relationship work for you and, if it doesn't, change your agent and/or the company – but remember to calculate carefully what the cost could be!

The Friendly Society manager

The roots of the Friendly Societies lie in the late eighteenth century, when they were set up as 'societies of good fellowship' to help members in difficulty. Since then they have evolved and been kept up to date. As a result of their pedigree they still enjoy exemption from income and corporation taxes on their life and endowment business up to certain levels. If you are a member, therefore, within certain limits, you can take out endowment assurance which enjoys complete freedom from tax in the fund in which the premiums are invested. There are other advantages, too, including having no shareholders (other than their members/investors perhaps), and limited risks. There is still a strong commitment to high standards of business ethics in the vast majority of Friendly Societies and you should be able to spot this quickly in your manager.

The 'independent' financial adviser and/or insurance broker

The chances are that these people will find you before you find them! Find out whether they really are independent or not! Frequently their services can be good, but you must be very aware that in most cases their remuneration will be by 'front-end loaded' commission. This means that the adviser – and very frequently this person is a self-employed salesman or woman pure and simple – gets his or her income as commission on the sale of a policy, which could be for a twenty-year term, mostly in one lump sum up-front as soon as you have signed the contract. In turn this means that most of your regular payments over the first year or more have gone straight into his or her pocket, and are not helping to build your fund. As you will probably already know, if you decide to cash the policy in early, say within the first five to ten years, you may have a nasty shock when you realise just how little of your money will be returned to you, partly because of the commission paid to the adviser, but also because of the administration and other expenses which the company has charged against it.

Insurance advisers come in two categories, tied or independent. This subject is covered in detail in Chapter 9. And, as has been said before, frequently they are more salespeople than advisers! You need to be very sure you understand whether or not the advice is being sales driven to too large a degree! It is equally vital for you to understand the difference between tied and independent advice. It could make all the difference to the value you get from your insurance and insurance-related savings and investments.

Another point of interest for you to remember is that some advisers will share their commission with you if you ask! It's worth a try . . .

To see how the cost implications of commission to advisers work out, study the information in the tables below. The first illustration shows the amounts of commission paid on a twenty-five-year endowment policy (£50 per month premium).

Paid to	Highest	Average	Lowest
Independent intermediary	£578	£498	£420
Authorised representative (*tied*)	£642	£570	£436

Source: LAUTRO 1992

The second illustration (overleaf) is a table of surrender values for different terms – given as an example only.

Year	Total premiums paid	Surrender value for term of	
		25 years	10 years
1	£1,200	£0	£160
2	£2,400	£0	£1,300
3	£3,600	£700	£2,600
4	£4,800	£1,900	£4,000
5	£6,000	£3,200	£5,600

Source: Savings and Investments Consumer Issues, Office of Fair Trading, 1992

Still on the subject of commission, and taken from the same report (Lautro 1992), a table of average commission or other charges for some of the most widely used products in savings and investments is shown on page 78.

There is no reason to deny yourself the benefits which could result in investment in insurance and insurance-related products, but it is as well to be aware of the real costs to you which need to be borne in mind when you are assessing the benefits. Chapter 9 addresses the subject of selecting a financial adviser. It spells out in detail the implications and offers you guidance on how to set about the process.

The unit trust and/or investment trust manager

He or she is generally accessed either by responding to advertising, direct mail and other promotional approaches, or through the bank or building society, or other financial adviser. He or she helps you to invest in the stock market via a 'pooled' investment product which offers the professional management you need to help make your money go further. Here again, though, you should be aware of the money you will be paying for the service. In terms of investment in unit trusts this includes up-front commission to the adviser when you buy the units or an equal deduction if you buy direct. This is money which is not available to you so you should recognise this – on purchase your investment is immediately reduced by around 5 per cent in most circumstances. There is also an annual management charge

Lump sum investments	Commission or fee
Unit trusts	3% commission
Investment trusts/other shares	1.65% stockbroker's fee (plus stamp duty 0.5%)
Personal equity plans (PEPs)	3% commission
National Savings, building society deposits, bank deposits	no commission or fee
Annuities	2% commission

Regular premium investments

Endowment assurance*	
10-year term	around 40% of first year's premium; 2.5% a year after initial period
25-year term	around 80% of first year's premium; 2.5% a year after initial period
Individual pensions*	
10-year term	around 30% of first year's premiums; 2.5% a year after initial period
25-year term	around 60% of first year's premiums; 2.5% a year after initial period
Unit trust regular savings schemes	3% commission on each payment
Investment trust savings schemes	variable, e.g. 1% charge on buying and selling, or 0.15% stockbroking charge plus 50p charge on each purchase (£5 on sale)
TESSAs	no commission or fee
National Savings	no commission or fee

* Commission is often paid on indemnity terms, i.e. all the commission covering the 'initial period' is paid up front when the contract is set up. The figures quoted are on this basis

on the value of your holding of around $1\frac{1}{2}$ per cent, which reduces the dividend accordingly. When you sell the units, too, you need to be aware of the difference between the buying and selling prices which, as indicated above, is usually around 5 per cent, but can vary, as can be seen from the daily newspapers listing the prices.

Investment trusts are different, but there is still a margin between the purchase and sale price, and you immediately lose the difference. An investment trust is a public company and if you invest with one you buy shares in the company itself, not directly related to the value of the shares held. Costs vary, but in general can be lower than those for unit trusts. As with unit trusts part of the benefit you are buying is the professional management of the company. Both unit and investment trusts are explained in more detail in Part 3 of this book.

It is a good idea to consider unit and/or investment trusts in any savings and investment portfolio, as they normally enable you to spread your risks in a prudent manner. They really provide a starter kit for investing in equities. Bear in mind, though, that the professional management of your money does come at a cost.

The solicitor

He or she is increasingly interested in getting your savings and investments business. Your solicitor will operate as an independent financial adviser. He or she is obliged to account for any commissions earned and to pay these over to you or credit them to you unless you and he or she have agreed otherwise, in writing (under Law Society rules). However, your solicitor may charge you for his or her time instead of getting commissions from the suppliers of insurance and investment-related products. Because financial services is not the mainstream of a solicitor's business it is important for you to check out carefully the training and competence credentials of anyone you are dealing with in the context of your savings and investments.

The accountant

He or she, like the solicitor, is increasingly trying to woo you as a client in relation to savings and investment. He or she will also operate as an independent financial adviser and the chances are you will be charged for time spent on your behalf. Remuneration for his or her services will probably be by fee, but could be by commission or a mixture of the two. Your accountant should also disclose to you if he or she is earning commission on your business and the amount of such commission. As with the solicitor, advising on financial services is not the mainstream activity of a chartered accountant, so you should ensure you check the training and competence credentials of anyone dealing with your savings and investments.

The stockbroker

He or she buys and sells shares on the Stock Exchange. He or she also deals in other investments such as gilts. You can find a stockbroker through the bank or by contacting the Stock Exchange. You may be asked to confirm a minimum amount of money which you want to invest before you are accepted as a client. Most stockbrokers are not interested in the small personal investor, but some are. Do be very sure that you are not a client on sufferance, treated as a second-class citizen by comparison with the wealthy private client or the prestigious and important corporate client!

These, then are the main money managers, sources of advice and service, with whom you can expect to deal. It is important to take the time and trouble to check out the personal chemistry between you before you give anyone your business. Very often the choice of establishment can be quite right but things have gone wrong because the two people involved, client and money adviser, were not on the same wavelength when it came to discussing matters and taking decisions. Remember it is your money, and also basically your responsibility to choose with whom you are dealing. Take enough time and trouble to ensure this decision is right for you. Then you can have a correct expectation that your money managers will be helping you to make more of your money. If in doubt, it is usually better to do nothing and keep your money somewhere safe until you are satisfied.

The role of the financial trade associations

As with other areas of business, trade associations have an important role to play in relation to the financial services market-place. Broadly speaking, there are trade associations representing the producers of the products (unit trusts, insurance policies, bank deposits etc.) in the various sectors, and trade associations representing the distributors (or retailers – in the main specialist salesmen and/or agents for the producers). Some aim for corporate membership (by the company) and some for individual membership (of the persons involved). Most operate with codes of practice, different formulae for particular sets of circumstances, some have ethical codes and special operations for encouraging education and training, or procedures for processing complaints against a member. Most have information services, and simple and practical leaflets and other information aids about their area of activity, and these vary from very good to indifferent. These are aimed separately at the member and at the consumer using the services of the member.

In the main the membership speaks for the majority of the prestigious, important and good operators in their sector. Most constantly try to influence their particular cowboys who are generally keen to stay out of membership for obvious reasons! The legitimate and responsible trade associations have varying degrees of success in their efforts to control the less scrupulous operators in the industry, but they are generally unremitting in their commitment to this. It is, alas, also a frequent practice for one or two major organisations in the sector to find it commercially beneficial to operate outside the membership of their sector trade association. Trade association codes of practice are generally well drafted and well intentioned; where there are gaps and/or weaknesses, these are in the levels of monitoring and strength of sanctions needed to give the code its necessary teeth in the interests of investor protection.

Trade associations have been up-front in their endeavours to help improve standards in the financial services sector. They are lucid, helpful and practical, paying particular attention to the need to lobby for their point of view in the many responses called for in relation to regulation. Frequently – and naturally – these responses will focus more on the priorities for the member and less on the priorities of the investor!

Trade associations that are important in the financial services industry are identified in Part 3 of this book.

CHAPTER 9

Choosing a Financial Adviser

To select a financial adviser who is suitable for your needs should be the simplest of processes, but very often it is not. Goodness knows there are enough of them about! It's quite frightening really to recognise just how many of them there are; well over a quarter of a million. You would imagine that it should be easy to choose the right one for you – but it isn't. Choosing the wrong one could cost you a lot of your money – others have found that it has cost them all of their money and they have ended up in serious debt. So how do you choose the right financial adviser?

That is what this chapter is all about.

And in coming to grips with this difficult question you should pick up some useful tips!

Tied or independent?

Fundamental to the operation of the Financial Services Act 1986, the piece of legislation which controls savings and investments, is the principle of what is called 'polarisation'. In simple terms this means that there are two types of selling systems – one that is tied and one that is independent. Note that they are called 'selling' systems, because both are focused rather too much on selling to you, rather than on advising the options which are best for you. But remember the cost of 'giving' you advice has to come from somewhere – a fee perhaps or a commission on what you buy.

Both systems have their advantages and, to get the best from the system, as usual, you should make yourself familiar with both before you choose. This is because, quite naturally, each has its limitations.

The tied adviser is tied or linked to a particular company (or group of companies). Each bank and nearly every building society is linked to just one insurance company (often their own in-house company), which each has chosen to provide you with services they themselves either don't cover or prefer not to promote. They too are tied. This means that your adviser, representing them, cannot offer you products from any other company. He or she is restricted to act only on behalf of that single organisation and the product range is, therefore, necessarily restricted. Also, the agent earns his or her income by selling you a product from his or her company. He or she may over-promote a product's benefits and is unlikely to promote an alternative savings product such as National Savings, TESSAs and possibly PEPs, where he or she will not get a direct return.

You may be perfectly happy with the service you are getting from that company, but you may be unaware of other products or services on the market which may offer you better value for your money and may be more appropriate in your case.

It is important, too, to remember that the tied agent is acting on behalf of the producer or the seller of the product and not for you, and that his or her income depends on persuading you to buy.

The alternative, the independent financial adviser, is acting for you, as *your* agent. They, too, need to earn a living from their clients as fees or as commissions on products sold, but they are obliged to give you best advice if they belong to FIMBRA. This means including appropriate recommendations on savings products, whether or not they obtain a commission.

There have been many instances of tied agents belonging to the sales forces of prestigious and famous companies going beyond their terms of reference and authorisation. As a result of this they may be offering products and services for which they are not authorised, and which are outside the scope of the company of which they are an authorised representative. Quite literally hundreds, if not thousands, of people have lost out by not understanding this point, indeed some have lost *all* their money and/or their homes. Compensation is available for losses incurred in respect of FIMBRA members (independent advisers) and normally in respect of tied agents, but only where they are acting within the scope of the Financial Services Act.

In contrast to the tied agent, therefore, the independent adviser should be advising you about a wider range of products and has the option of searching the whole market in order to put the best and most practical options in front of you. The independent is not limited in relation to choice, although in practice options put in front of you could be drawn from, say, ten organisations which the adviser thinks may be particularly appropriate to your needs. IFAs may or may not be authorised to handle clients' money, yet this does not indicate that those who do are more honest, but they do have to observe more strict compliance monitoring. If an IFA is not authorised to handle cash, all cheques for investments should be made payable by the investor to the product company – for the further protection of you, the investor.

The most important point to remember is that the independent adviser is acting for you, as your agent.

There is no right answer to the question of whether to take tied or independent advice. Both may give you entirely suitable information. But you do need to be clear as to *which* type of advice you are getting.

Paying for financial advice – fees or commissions?

It is likely that both the tied agent and the independent adviser will be remunerated by commission from the organisations whose products you will be buying. While many do not think it is important to know the extent of the commission the adviser will be getting, it is useful to find out. Indeed, as from the beginning of 1995, new rules will ensure you are told the exact facts as to commissions and other charges deducted from your money before it is put to work for you.

If you are dealing with an independent adviser you should

find this easy. It is not as simple to find out from a tied agent, but you can try. Do remember though that, in the main, you are talking about buying a long-term saving or investment product, so you should not be too taken aback in relation to the extent of the commission the agent will be getting – and you do need to remember that this has to cover other costs as well, for example administration and selling costs. Quite literally, obtaining the best value for money can often mean choosing the most expensive option which will perform and suit your needs best over the long term. For substantial transactions an IFA may agree a fee which is lower than the commission which he or she might otherwise obtain and you would expect to benefit from the difference.

There is another way of getting financial advice and this is by paying for it. This is by payment of fees, similar to the service you get from your solicitor or your accountant. This means that your adviser will be paid for his or her time by a fee, the terms of which should be negotiated before any relationship is confirmed. If you do elect to pay fees for financial advice, you may be in for a nasty surprise because you will be quoted at the rate of £60 to £150 per hour for the time involved. But don't go into shock ... The commission payments made to your tied or independent adviser could amount to them helping themselves to more of your money in the long term (see tables on pages 76-8). There is no such thing as free advice.

There is, however, a further point about the commission system which needs to be made. Many advisers will argue that it is in your interests because it is free. This is because the adviser only gets paid if you buy something! These advisers will press the point that the fee-based adviser always gets paid – whether you buy or not. Some will also hint that those who get paid fees are those who are unsuccessful at earning a living on the commission system! In addition, you have to remember that the commission also covers many of the administration and other costs which the adviser has to bear – the commission earned does not really constitute the adviser's 'take home pay'!

Having said all the above, the popularity of the fees system is growing and could well provide you with an attractive option – as long as you have the self-discipline not to ask for unnecessary meetings and go to any meeting with your fee-based adviser properly briefed with the information you need, and the facts the adviser will need and expect to get from you. This should help to keep the fees reasonable.

Many independent advisers today will also offer you a system which includes both fees and commissions.

Where do you start looking for financial advice?

There is no shortage of sources of advice on finance, but what is important is to recognise that you need the source to be professional, trained, competent and authorised. There are hair-raising (and true!) stories of financial advisers using millions of pounds of funds collected from bona fide investors, to try out new types of racing systems! This is just one example of the horror stories reported regularly in the national and specialist press. There are, alas, many others. It is important, therefore, to be sure where you stand with regard to a potential financial adviser. Most important of all, check that your adviser is authorised. Indeed, under the Financial Services Act 1986 all advisers must either be authorised through one of the Self-Regulatory Organisations (SROs) or operate through a Recognised Professional Body (RBP). Professional specialist advisers belong to SROs. Solicitors and chartered accountants belong to their RPBs, and may be regulated for investment business under their procedures. All insurance brokers have to be in membership of the Insurance Brokers Registration Council which is also recognised, for the purposes of the Act, as an RPB.

All financial advisers need to display their authorisation details on their letterhead, business cards, premises etc., so you can tell clearly their status (e.g. whether tied or independent) and, if tied, which product company they represent.

It is most important to know whether or not you are dealing with an authorised adviser, as only authorised advisers are covered by compensation and restitution arrangements. If you are in doubt consult the Securities and Investments Board (SIB), the lead regulator, which maintains a register of all authorised firms and individuals (see Part 3).

How do you choose?

How do you find out about your financial adviser, about his or her track record and past performance?

One important fact for you to remember, with particular reference to the tied area, is that there is a high turnover of staff. They tend to enter the financial services field and then, if they are not successful, or producing sufficient volume of business to keep their company happy, they leave in a relatively short period of time, say two years. Put cynically, they are used for their address books and the contacts they can deliver as sales leads. When their usefulness is finished they are 'disposed of' to make way for others. This position, though, is changing because of strict new rules on training and competence which are being introduced by the regulators. This, in turn, means that it will be more expensive for an insurance company, for example, to maintain its sales force of tied agents and, indeed, over the last twelve months, from November 1992 to November 1993, the overall number of such company representatives or 'tied' agents has reduced from 170,219 to 131,922. However, a major insurance company will still have a sales force of several thousand agents. As a result of the new training and competence regulations there should, in the future, be more stability in the system. The lower rate of staff turnover and sound training should also, in due course, deliver higher quality results to you in terms of higher and more consistent standards of advice. It should also hopefully lower your costs and give better value for money.

Independent financial advisers, by contrast, tend to be people who have longer experience in the industry, decide they liked it and have stayed in it, over many years. They are principals of their own firms and have a self-interest in building up their businesses by maintaining an on-going relationship with each client, based on delivering consistently good advice. Their training requirements now mean (with very few exceptions) that they have to pass an independent professional qualification (the Financial Planning Certificate) to obtain full registration status.

So, in terms of finding out about your potential financial adviser, here are some tips. They are related to the preparation of a Reverse Fact Find, to mirror the Fact Find which you filled in in Chapter 6 and which the adviser has to prepare if you are likely to be a new client.

Reverse Fact Find – or 'Know Your Adviser'

1. Are they tied or independent?

2. Are they authorised by FIMBRA, LAUTRO, IMRO or an RPB? (See Part 3.)

3. How long has your potential adviser been in the industry and for whom have they worked? Go back 5–7 years.

4. Can he or she point to any client who will endorse the usefulness of his or her advice – a satisfied customer whom you could trust, and whom *you* can contact for a reference?

5. If the potential adviser is an independent, can you talk with a product provider he or she has used over many years? This may be an insurance or unit trust company, for example.

6. Does the adviser have a 'clean record' in terms of the regulators and trade associations? Has he or she, for example, been called in front of their regulator on disciplinary matters? Try to get the answer to this question in writing.

7. Ask whether he or she is covered for professional indemnity insurance?

8. Are they authorised to handle cash or are all cheques to be made payable by you to a product company (this helps to prevent fraud, but does not ensure the quality of advice)?

9. Will they give you everything possible in writing?

10. Ask the potential adviser the following questions, which are identified by Dr Julian Farrand, the Insurance Ombudsman, in his 1992 Report.
   (a) Whose agent are you?
   (b) How much commission will you get from this transaction?

(c) What charges will be made for managing my money?

(d) Will I do better with the building society?

(e) Could I lose money?

(f) What is your persistency record (financial jargon for 'How many of your customers jacked their policies in early')?

(g) How soon will the surrender value equal premiums paid?

(h) Why are you advising me to buy this particular policy/investment?

In setting out this list of questions, you may well be faced by reactions from your potential adviser which may vary from surprise, through hurt to even outrage! The bona fide adviser, however, will have nothing to lose in answering them honestly. Remember, you are the buyer and it is your money you are being asked to part with. It is your responsibility to protect it as much as you possibly can.

It is possible that you may also get some useful background information from some of the specialist trade papers. It's worth having a look! They are identified in Part 3 of this book.

Make sure, through careful enquiry, that you pick a financial adviser who is well above the average in terms of experience, ability and ethical standards. Talk the matter over with people you trust in terms of their financial acumen and understanding of the financial markets. It is much better to be safe, rather than sorry ... Don't deal with anyone you have not checked out carefully, as this could easily affect the return you get from your money.

Is it better to find a financial adviser or to go it alone?

Even five years ago this was a relevant question. In 1994 it is not. If you wish to go it alone, you can of course do so. But do be aware that you will be taking a substantial risk by doing so.

In today's sophisticated financial markets which are so fast moving, it is not possible for even the most sophisticated investor, someone who may read the *Financial Times* from cover to cover every day, to ensure that he or she is sufficiently knowledgeable and up to date to make the correct, cost-effective decisions on savings and investments. Belatedly the industry has recognised also the high priority which needs to be given to training and competence. The established 'core knowledge' requirements for any financial adviser today – whether tied or independent – cover specific requirements in the following areas:

- investments and investment planning;
- personal financial planning;
- estate planning;
- business assurance and corporate planning;
- retirement planning;
- mortgage and capital raising;
- taxation;
- products and funds on the market from which choices can be made (a vast and complex range of many hundreds of options);
- compliance (regulatory requirements) and the detail of the Financial Services Act.

At first glance you may think that many of these areas are not relevant to your needs, but to operate your own financial plan without the aid of a competent financial adviser you need to have at least some knowledge of these areas and the interaction between them.

Some important points for you to bear in mind before you choose a financial adviser, and even if you are thinking of going it alone, are as follows.

- In order to make your savings and investments work hard and effectively for you, you have to ensure that you have the *right level of quality in the advice* you are given.

- Before you can be sure of the quality of advice, you need to ensure that the *right level and quality of knowledge* is present in the adviser you are considering entrusting with your business.

- *It is only when the necessary level of knowledge is present in*

91

your adviser that the quality of advice can be delivered, and this can then be underpinned by the selection of the right options to satisfy your objectives.

In the tied sector, where only the products and services of a single organisation are on offer, the 'core knowledge' threshold is established at the level of the Financial Planning Certificate of the Chartered Insurance Institute, Part 1. In the independent sector, where the products and services of the industry can be reviewed to enable the choice of the right and most suitable products and services for your purposes, the standard is established at the complete Financial Planning Certificate to include Part 1 and also Parts 2 and 3. This means that an independent will have a more substantial and deeper level of knowledge to underpin the advice you will be receiving.

Finally, remember, whatever advice you are given, before committing yourself it is often very useful to discuss that advice with friends or relations who may have some financial knowledge to double check that what you have been told stands up to examination. Also, it is usually sensible not to act immediately on advice you have been given. Reflect on it for at least forty-eight hours. Don't be hustled into quick decisions just because the adviser wants to close the sale. Good advisers will not push you!

How to work with an adviser

Do remember that it is your responsibility to brief your adviser thoroughly. Any results he or she will be able to achieve will be affected at least to some degree by the effectiveness of your briefing. Make sure that you don't lose out.

Here are some questions to ask yourself and/or your financial adviser in relation to taking decisions about savings and investments.

- **What is the level of risk I am taking with my money?** See Part 3 of this book to assess the upside and downside of the particular options which interest you.

- **When can I expect to cash in this investment (or policy) and be sure that I will get all my money back?** With deposit-based options (such as banks and building societies) the answer is related to the terms of the particular product, but for insurance-based options you may need to be persuasive to get the information and, even then, your question can only be answered in part. However, some information is better than no information! In the case of the equity-based options (such as shares, unit and investment trusts), the answer is even more difficult to determine. However, it is worth persisting and getting as many details as you can *before* you make your choice. Part 3 of this book provides information on which you can build.

- **Is this product/option the best one for me?** Are there others on the market which could be better? Can I be sure? For example, it could be that you have some ten years or more of pension contributions in your employers' occupational pension scheme and you are being asked to transfer these funds into another, new scheme. If this scheme is put in front of you by a bank it could easily mean that you only get one option to choose from. It is important to establish whether or not this is the position. In wise buying it is never prudent to make a choice without reviewing more than one option! Indeed the issue of Pension Transfers has been much in the news of recent months. The important point emerging is your need to have the fullest information possible before you make a decision relative to your pension.

- **Does the advice I am getting constitute 'best advice' under the Financial Services Act?** Can I get a signed statement from you as my adviser to this effect? It is a very reasonable request to ask for this comfort from your financial adviser. Don't be put off by any excuses. If he or she is not prepared to sign a suitable statement to the effect that they are prepared to stand by their advice to you, this is a real warning that all is not as it should be!

- **What happens if something goes wrong?** What if the adviser goes broke or if the investment needs to be realised quickly?

A word of warning if you are of mature years

Anyone over retirement age is particularly vulnerable to financial services selling. This group can be specifically targeted by unscrupulous, smooth-talking advisers. Many people start to lose some self-confidence as they grow older. The really smart person acknowledges this and plans accordingly not to expose themselves to risks, wherever they may come from.

CHAPTER 10

Tricks of the Trade – Beware!

In all areas of marketing there are some practices which emerge and prove worthwhile, in terms of financial rewards, to those whose standards of business ethics are somewhat lower than one would like to see. In most cases the techniques are fine-tuned so that it is difficult to outlaw them because the practice involved is not downright illegal. It is as well to be aware of the practices so that you are protected by knowledge and can recognise if you are the target and likely to be at risk!

This chapter aims to give you that necessary information.

There are many tricks of the trade with regard to financial services. It is virtually impossible to identify all of them and new ones are being added constantly. Here, however, are some of the most obvious ones to look out for.

Tricks of language and presentation

Use of the word 'guarantee'

Always be very, very wary if anyone tells you that a return on a saving or investment product is 'guaranteed'. Some products are more or less guaranteed to retain their initial values, but not all are and sometimes the word 'guarantee' can be used in a misleading way. Check precisely what is guaranteed and under what circumstances the guarantee may not be total.

Use of the word 'safe'

Here again, the premise on which the word is used needs to be examined most carefully! Safe often means low risk – not always *no risk*!

Use of graphs, projected future returns and the like

Check that the figures used and featured match the geometry of the graph ... Frequently they don't! The figures may paint a much more modest picture than the graph portrays!

Beware of projections

They can be misleading in spite of all the regulators' efforts to ensure their accuracy, especially in the current economic climate. Many return rates are falling and may not match returns actually obtained over recent past years.

Tricks of advice and selling

'Churning'

This is the jargon term used when your adviser suggests you change one set of savings and investment products for another. Each time he or she buys or sells on your behalf it is very likely your adviser is earning money on the transaction, which could be in the range of 2–5 per cent of your premium, sometimes more, sometimes less. Each time you change your investment you have to allow extra time for your money to recover from the cost incurred in making the change! So ask at the outset what the charges are and satisfy yourself as far as you can that the suggested changes – and charges involved – are justified.

Stockbrokers and managed portfolio companies have also been known to yield to the temptation to 'churn', so remember this if you are dealing with one!

'Cross-selling'

This is the jargon term used when your name and address is 'sold' to another company (it could be in the financial sector or in another, totally unrelated, sector, anything from carpets, time-share to electronic equipment). Another 'strange' company, which has targeted you as a potential customer for them, will then approach you with junk mail, involving seemingly unforgettable and unrepeatable 'special offers' and the like. Today there are ways you can protect yourself from such mailings, but experience would seem to indicate that people are reluctant to do so. So be on your guard and the best advice is normally to tear up all unsolicited mail.

'Vanity selling'

This is when you are informed that the special offer is being made to only the 'top' people in your field!

Every single citizen in the country is logged on several computer systems, with a disturbing amount of personal information held about them. And this is all in spite of the Data Protection Act 1984 which is supposed to protect us from such abuse by laying down principles of fair obtaining of information to be observed by commerce. Some commentators also believe that European legislation could well open the floodgates and erode such protection as we currently enjoy.

Cold phone calling

Sometimes you may also be 'cold called' over the telephone to buy a financial service in the same way that double glazing is sold. The safe advice is to terminate all such calls immediately.

'Switch selling'

Here a particular product is promoted. It sounds good and so you respond. But the offer is used rather as a 'loss leader', and frequently there is persuasive selling to use the lead to you in order to switch the sale and to sell you something completely different! And likewise, if a free gift is involved, beware – it's an inducement for you to buy on the spur of the moment, with the cost in the price of the product, and you might often regret the transaction at your leisure.

Advertising

It is important to know how to read between the lines with all advertising, direct mail and promotion. Check that every source featured is one you can really respect. For example, the fact that a unit trust company has been awarded a prize for a good performance by a specialist paper may mean something, but more often it is a cosmetic 'plus' chosen specially to impress and does not stand up to any really robust examination. Check, too, that any graph matches the figures in relation to scale and be very wary if the word 'guarantee' is used. It can rarely be justified.

When alarm bells should start ringing

In relation to the advertising of financial products and services, alarm bells should start ringing in your head if you notice any of the following.

- There is an absence of 'health warnings' – for example, a statement that past performance is not a guide to future prospects.

- Past performance records do not contain the relevant timespan –for example collective investments such as unit trusts should provide figures to compare with the five-year figure laid down by the regulator, in this case LAUTRO.

- Promises are over-extravagant or misleading – for example 'In ten years this could lead you . . .' is meaningless unless the realistic conditions under which the performance can be achieved are set out clearly and fully.

- There is any 'back-tracking' – for example if the claim is 'If you had bought this PEP in 1974 . . .' when PEPs were not available at that time! 'Back-tracking' is now forbidden by the Financial Services Regulators.

- It is suggested that the virtue in the product is unique – for example 'The investment we put into gilts is guaranteed by the Bank of England'. This is meaningless because the bank guarantees to repay gilts at their face value, and to repay interest, not that the value of any particular investment by a particular investor will not fall in value.

- The name/logo of the self-regulatory organisation of which the company is a member does not appear. Relevant logos include those of LAUTRO and FIMBRA. It is illegal for the company to carry on investment business without membership of its relevant SRO.

The example on pages 100-1 shows a press advertisement by Jones Brown Limited (a fictitious FIMBRA member) to illustrate the main areas of possible complaint against bad advertising. Obviously one simple advertisement is unlikely to contravene all the areas, but two or three rule breaches have certainly been seen at once. This example should give you some idea of the danger signs to look out for in advertising.

On page 102 is an illustration of a piece of direct mail, which illustrates the sometimes insidious and misleading nature of this type of promotion. To the recipient it often appears as a *personal* letter, that arrives on the potential investor's breakfast table with other personal mail. Often there is an implication that the advertiser knows the recipient and his or her personal financial circumstances, for example.

The golden rule to remember is the harder someone tries to sell you something, the warier you ought to be, for if high pressure is necessary then the product is unlikely to be good. However, despite all the warnings it should be emphasised that most financial advisers – be they independent or tied – are honest people and the regulators are working hard to banish all rogues from the industry as soon as they are identified.

HOME OWNER?

WE GUARANTEE [1]
TO INCREASE
YOUR INCOME

If you are an elderly house owner, we can help unlock the capital tied up in your home and turn it into income – tax free. Half of your money will be invested in leading unit trusts giving capital growth. **[2]** The other half helps earn you a high regular monthly income. **[3]**

[4] We can reduce your income tax bill and as a home owner with large outgoings you know how much you value the security of a high regular income and capital growth.

If you had invested in 1975 in a PEP scheme such as the one we are recommending for you now, your **[5]** capital would have increased 425%.

[6] Get your advice from Jones Brown, an independent financial adviser, rather than from an appointed representative who works for his life insurance company rather than for you.

Jones Brown Limited is a member of FIMBRA which guarantees protection to investors under the Financial Services Act. **[7]**

FIMBRA
MEMBER

Jones Brown Limited

[8] The largest specialist home owners' income advisers in the country

Pitfalls in press advertising

This case study shows a press advertisement by Jones Brown Limited (a fictitious FIMBRA member) to illustrate the main areas of possible complaint against bad advertising. Obviously one simple advertisement is unlikely to contravene all the areas but two or three rule breaches have been seen at once.

1. **'Guarantee'** misused.

2. No **health warning** that the value of the investment can fall as well as rise.

3. **Misleading** as it does not make clear the income is a withdrawal of capital.

4. **Product Problem** What product could do both successfully?

5. **Backtracking** into a fictitious situation as PEP did not exist in 1975.

6. **Tendentious** Knocking copy against tied agents.

7. **Misleading** use of the FIMBRA *symbol* as a guarantee of consumer protection rather than an SRO identifier.

8. **Untrue** or impossible to prove.

Direct Mail Horrors

Today direct mail, if not used with discretion, can provide the most insidious and misleading type of advertising. To the recipient it often appears as a <u>personal</u> letter that arrives on the potential investor's breakfast table with other personal mail. Often there is an implication that the advertiser knows the recipient and his or her personal financial circumstance, for example:

'An exciting investment linked to high-interest building society account for anyone seeking high income, capital growth, or both

U.K. interest rates have fallen to their lowest level for 10 years. However, I have some very good news for you. Today I am able to offer you the opportunity to profit from a unique investment, linked to a High-Interest Building Society Account that allows you to plan not only for capital growth, but also for high income, if required.'

or disturbing the recipient about his investment caution:

'Inflation – what does it really mean?

How are your Bank or Deposit Account investments currently performing? Over the last few months you may have moved a proportion of your money into a Bank Deposit or High Interest Account, as have many of my other clients. A Deposit Account is seen as a "safe" refuge for money in the current investment climate.'

and exclusivity is professed:

'This offer is exclusive to you, as a client of Smith Brown & Company. I believe that you, like many of my other clients,'

then an 'income' is offered which is not really an income but a withdrawal of the investors own capital:

'If you do want to take an income, you can withdraw from the Existing Growth Fund Portfolio, up to 10% each year on a monthly basis, free of any individual liability to basic rate income tax or Capital Gains Tax, and your investment could still show handsome capital growth as well.'

and lastly the whole deal is 'guaranteed' by the Bank of England.

'And the portion of your investment which we put into "gilts" on your behalf is guaranteed by the Bank of England.'

To top it off the FIMBRA symbol is used as the guarantee of safety rather than the SRO identifier:

FIMBRA

Smith & Jones are members of the Financial Intermediaries, Managers and Brokers Regulatory Association (FIMBRA) which means that when you invest you know you have the guarantee of safety provided by the recent Financial Services Act.

How to spot a con-man (or woman) and how to avoid fraud

We can all become the victims of a con-man (or woman) and fraud, so don't be ashamed if it happens to you! There are, however, some golden rules which you can observe to make the risk less likely.

- The more you put into a single scheme the bigger the risk you are taking.
- The higher the reward you are promised, more than the usual, the higher is the likelihood that you may be dealing with a con-man or woman and could be exposed to fraud.
- The more secretive the deal, the more it is claimed to be 'informal', an offer you can't refuse, one only hand-picked, 'privileged' clients are being told about, the more it could be less than it appears and perhaps positively 'dodgy'.
- The request to make out a cheque to the individual adviser without evidence of bona fides with regard to the investment can loudly spell out the warning 'Be very careful – back off'. Don't make cheques out to individuals, only to the principal company. If possible, use credit cards for further protection in the case of first premiums etc. Always, yes *always*, get a second opinion from someone independent before you buy. This is one of the best defences against fraud. Never ask the salesperson to recommend someone to you to confirm his or her advice on a specific choice. If possible, seek out a friend, someone whose financial acumen you respect, and discuss the matter in general with them – remembering always that under the Act the specific advice or recommendation must always come from someone authorised to give it.

Remember, the con-man or woman will naturally seem more honest than the ordinary adviser – they wouldn't be a successful 'con' otherwise!

For a con-man or woman or fraud to be successful they need to persuade you that the investment is better and safer than it is, also that the risk is less than it really is. There are plenty of clever people about who will try to persuade you of this. If it sounds too good to be true, watch out. Watch out, too, for the omission of vital information. Quite often the would-be con-artist or fraudster will either tell you lies, or omit to tell you something important, or even dismiss vital information about the deal in the small print by telling you that it is irrelevant or unimportant. The most successful fraudsters often masquerade as pillars of respectability – remember Robert Maxwell!

Fraud and risk

Some risks are almost impossible to avoid. Even the safest of investments (such as most forms of National Savings) risk the erosion of your money through inflation. Others, like equity investments (unit and investment trusts, stocks and shares, for example) risk the value of your assets going down as well as up because of the turbulence of the world's international money markets and economic conditions.

For most methods of savings and investments there is some level of protection available through compensation and redress schemes. But with fraud there is little chance of getting your money back, as can be evidenced from the many media reports that appear week on week. In this context it is as well to bear in mind that fraud is currently running at record levels (by the end of August 1992 the total known UK fraud had reached an all-time high of £445 million for the year). It is, after all, of little comfort to you to know that the plausible salesperson from whom you bought those dodgy investments is now enjoying Her Majesty's hospitality! You have still lost your money . . .

Remember always that for fraud to succeed you have to be a willing victim!

CHAPTER 11

Keeping Track of Your Money

It is of the greatest importance with regard to your savings and investments that you know what is going on and that you are keeping track of your money. This is not only important from the point of view of fraud or things going wrong, but is crucial in making sure your money is working hard for you. It is vital to keep abreast of what your tax implications may be and how the overall matter of tax affects you. After all, there is no point in putting your money into an investment which may offer you attractive returns only to find that tax has eroded much of the gains and to recognise, too late, that you would have been better advised to settle for an investment with a more modest return, but which offered you greater tax effectiveness.

Inflation and its effects also have to be taken into account in this context.

Who keeps you informed about what is happening to your money? How do you find out?

The person whose prime responsibility it is to keep you informed about what is happening to your money is you. If you have a financial adviser, for example an independent financial adviser (such as a stockbroker or an insurance broker), or even the representative of your bank or building society, they will have systems in place which should update you – but it is up to you to check on their frequency and adequacy. Also, be very sure that you won't be charged without your prior approval for any special requirements you may place on them to keep you up to date. On the other hand, you may feel quite happy to pay for the additional service as it could represent real value for your money.

I have said before in this book – and there are no apologies for saying it again – you need to check regularly on how your savings and investments are performing. Try to ensure that you are updated at least quarterly, but preferably monthly. It will pay you handsomely. A simple formula would be to get a regular updating service built in by your adviser, and then do your own sums for the interim periods. This shouldn't be too difficult, costly or time-consuming. Very soon you should find it quite routine.

Don't forget, too, that when you are assessing just what you are worth, you have to take into consideration more than just the performance of any savings and investment portfolio you have. You need to be sensitive as to how your insurance policy bonus may be moving as a result of the prevailing economic climate. You need, too, to be realistic about whether the value of your home is going up or down in relation to any mortgage you may have. In addition, it may be as well to examine whether your current mortgage is the right one for you and if you need to change this – for example to transfer from an endowment mortgage to a repayment mortgage (you will need to find out first how much it will cost and what benefits may be lost in order to change to cheaper repayments). You need, too, to be familiar with the current interest rates.

It will be useful to fill in a worksheet, like the example opposite, to help you keep track of your finances. You should either get one from your adviser or prepare one for yourself, updating it as necessary, but preferably every quarter.

Investment worksheet

NAME: MR AND MRS J. SOAP

PORTFOLIO OBJECTIVE: Reasonable income and growth prospects

VALUATION DATE: 4 January 1994

PURCHASE DATE 29 January 1991

UNIT TRUSTS/SHARES/OTHER INVESTMENTS

[Specify under different categories, for example:]

UK Gilts Convertible & Gilt – Unit Trusts or Shares

Purchase date 29 January 1991: 39,340.8000 Bloggs Convertible Trust

Current Price .5974

Current Value (£) 23,502

Original Cost of Holding (£) 17,500

Gross Yield (%) 5.6

Gross Income (£) 1,316.12

[Then, if you add the same information for all the other securities you hold, you should have an important list to update.]

[The important bottom line should include:]

TOTAL VALUE OF THE PORTFOLIO £_____

CURRENT VALUE £_____

ORIGINAL COST OF HOLDING £_____

[You will then know exactly how much you have made (or lost) in the period during which you have held the portfolio.]

Checklist for keeping track of your money

A good weekly discipline:

If something unusual has occurred, entailing a larger than expected payment into or out of your account, make a note of it in your diary . . .

Some useful tips and hints for a good monthly discipline:

- Go through your diary and transfer any notes of the unusual payments into and out of your accounts.

- On a small piece of paper, suitable for putting in your wallet or keeping in your diary, make a note of the following:

  1. Cash resources: Money in your current and deposit bank and/or building society accounts.

  2. Other
       money you may have in other accounts
       unit trusts, investment trusts, other saving and investments at approximate valuation
       very approximate valuations for property, including your home, car etc.

  3. Information you may have about any large payment you may have to make, for example, tax, business rates, your holiday.

  4. Finally, total up the sum of all your resources, and review this month on month. Keep this information handy so you can see how your financial affairs are progressing.

More formal disciplines:

Using the information in this book (and other information you may have), make a firm decision to review matters more formally quarterly and annually. If you have a financial adviser, get his or her help with this.

Moving your money around – is it worth while?

Here again, this is very much a matter for you to decide. Through reading this book you should be very aware that every time you do move your money around, switching from this unit trust to that insurance product, for example, others are making a 'turn' out of you which costs you money. This can operate both on the selling and the buying functions, so the performance of your new investment has to be that much better, or left to work that much longer, to make up for the commission and / or fees you have paid out. And this can be the case even if you buy direct from, say, your favourite unit trust company. This is because the unit trust company, while paying commission to your adviser, will not allow you any of that commission if you buy from the company direct.

Having said that, sometimes there are good reasons why you will want to change your investments. If you keep well in mind the fact that investment is a long-term business, and that moving your money around costs you more than you might think, you will be in the right frame of mind to take your decision. But be careful. For example, if you have bought an endowment policy (see Part 3) you will find that it will begin to grow more after the first few years (when you have had to pay the commission 'load' on the policy), so you should recognise that it is important to keep the policy until it reaches its maturity date because that is when the final bonus is added – yielding to temptation and cashing it in even one or two months early so that you can invest the proceeds in something else could mean that you lose out seriously. On the other hand, it is possible to 'swop' investments around using the various share and unit trust exchange schemes which are provided as incentives from time to time.

Another factor which you should consider is that investments which you may have bought in the past and are based on capital growth, may need now to be switched to an income base, because you are anticipating a drop in your income. But do try to keep capital growth above inflation, even if income is the first priority for you. This needs to be discussed in detail with your adviser so that you know all the options before you take a decision.

The tax implications (dealt with later in this chapter) are always an important factor to bear in mind before you decide to move your money around. Each time you sell investments you incur either a gain or a loss. Sometimes this is a positive reason for selling and putting your money into another investment. If you are making a gain, remember the capital gains tax implications (currently tax year 1993/4, unchanged for 1994/5), after adjustment for inflation – the indexation allowance – the first £5,800 of capital gains in a tax year is tax free, thereafter gains are subject to tax after adjustment for inflation since the investments were purchased; tables setting out the inflation factors are published monthly in the *Daily Telegraph* and the *Investor's Chronicle*). In the case of a loss, this can be set against gains made over previous years, so it could make good sense to get rid of an unpopular investment which is losing money, and set the loss against the gains you may have made on the sale of the business you built up over the years, for example, and decided to sell recently.

It is as well to draw attention to the potential in 'bed and breakfast deals' at this point. Towards the end of a tax year, you may be showing an unrealised loss on one or two potentially promising investments, while at the same time you have a capital gains tax liability above the current exemption limit on realised profits. In these circumstances it can pay you to 'bed and breakfast' the loss-makers, i.e. sell them to establish your loss and then buy them back the next day. This should help to reduce your tax bill for the year!

The essential questions to ask yourself before you decide to move your investments around are as follows.

- Why do I think it may be a good idea?
- What are the gains and/or losses involved? Now? In the future?
- How much of my money will be used in making the change?
- What do, or might, I lose by leaving things as they are?

Cashing in – is it a good idea?

Cashing in your investments (when you don't have to) can be a good idea if you need the cash for something which offers a better return. For example, you may want to buy a larger house, a share in a business or even to buy into the wholesale money markets where the larger sum you can put on deposit with the bank or building society will earn you a higher rate of interest. Cashing in can also be a good idea if you have decided that you are really uncomfortable dealing with the intangible aspects of investments and want to feel that your money is in a haven which you believe is more secure, such as a bank or building society. In this case, read Chapter 12 on consumer protection carefully, where you will note the sobering fact that money on deposit in banks and building societies is really less protected than that in the investment industry. The track record of things going wrong with such investments is not as poor as it is in some sectors of the financial services industry, but there is a risk all the same. Be aware of it.

There are two other important points to note with regard to cashing in your savings and investments.

- In the case of insurance policies be very sure that you won't be losing out. It is sad but true that most policy-holders are not aware of the poor returns they will get if they cash their policies in in the early years of their investment, rather than waiting until the maturity date of the policy.

- Check whether, if you realise your investment, this will incur capital gains tax (the tax you have to pay if you exceed the limit allowed on the profit you have received from the sale of assets or other possessions – see pages 110, 115-16) or other tax liabilities, to ensure that it is going to be really worthwhile, unless you have a compelling reason to cash in that investment.

Who tells you when to sell your investments?

This is the real crux of savings and investments. When you want to *buy* the financial services industry seeks you out ... after all they do have vested interests in selling you their products and services. But, when it comes to advising their clients on when to sell, they seem to disappear like melted snow and may not be there to advise you! It is indeed truly difficult to tell when the market is at its peak. If we could tell that we should all be multi-millionaires – if we took even a fleeting interest in managing our money well. But the fundamental truth remains the same – when it comes to deciding when to sell, the chances are you're on your own.

There is one further fact which it is also important for you to recognise. And that is when you are advised to sell (if you are), it pays to look once, twice, forwards and backwards, before you take the advice. One of the tricks of the trade, as described in Chapter 10, is churning, when the financial adviser advises you to sell your investments and to buy others which, according to him or her, will serve your interests better. In many cases your adviser is thinking more of his or her pocket than of yours! So, at the very least, ask sharp questions to determine just how much it is in their financial interest to give you this advice, and at least try hard to ensure that any financial benefits are shared with you!

Having said that, nothing remains the same in this volatile world. Therefore, it is as well that you keep your own finger on the pulse of the economy. This is very easy to do. Indeed it can be said that it is actually hard to escape from the economic news of the day. The simplest way to start is to read the money pages of your national and local papers, and favourite magazines. The personal finance articles of your daily and Sunday newspapers are very useful. The BBC Radio 4 programme *Money Box* also gives a very useful update on personal finance matters twice weekly.

Then you should also check up on how the financial indices are moving. These are really the barometers of the economic health of the nation. The most accessible of these is the *Financial Times* (FT) 100 Index (the Footsie). It is published daily in the newspapers and you can also refer to its movements day by day on the television Teletext service. Another is the FT 30 Share Index, which tracks the thirty largest 'blue-chip' shares day by day, and you can check up on this, too, on the TV and in your newspaper.

As a rule of thumb, if the Footsie loses more than fifty points in a day and doesn't recover them reasonably quickly (say over a week), there is an underlying serious situation which you should take note of. If there is a serious drop, say 100 points within a week, this is naturally immediately more serious. So, what do you do in this case? The answer is that you must look at the matter objectively and make a positive decision as to whether or not to act. Even a decision to do nothing at all can be a positive decision in this context.

In order to review the matter you should take the following into consideration. The first lesson to be learnt about investment is that growth is necessarily a long-term business. If there is a chance of leaving your investments where they are and sitting out the current crisis, then you should do that. On the other hand, you need to be canny, and to be sensitive to the long-term economic climate. For example, when the property market started to slide in the late 1980s and early 1990s, many people hung on to their property in the hope that the property market would recover – and lost out as a result. Those who were wise were those who had recognised that it was certainly not inevitable that property prices would rise and rise, that the prices had exploded in earlier years and that the logical reaction would be for the market to fall back to a more realistic level. As a result they sold property when the market might have been some 5 to 10 per cent off its all-time high, and also bought, soon afterwards, in the new lower level market, thereby trading-up on their houses without losing out!

Your next rule of thumb is to recognise that you know as much as most others about when to sell. Don't shy away from the decision-taking. If you feel the time is right, take action, bearing in mind the long-term implications of your decision – but do your homework. Don't rely on tips, hunches, instincts or feelings alone. Above all, don't be panicked into selling – or into buying either.

The tax implications of selling

Tax can drastically affect the return you get from your investments and it can also provide the answer to the question of whether you should sell. It is important, therefore, to know the effect of the tax position you are in before you can judge the merit of any investment you may be considering, whether the issue is buying or, more particularly, selling.

For example, let us say that you are paying higher rate tax and you select an investment costing you £100,000 and paying you an income of 10 per cent a year (a very good rate at the time of writing). You chose this investment over one which would not pay you any income but should, you hope, give you a capital gain of 8 per cent a year.

At first glance, since both figures are both before payment of tax, your choice looks a wise one. On further inspection, however, you would have been wiser if you had chosen the second option. This is because paying Higher Rate Tax, currently at 40%, reduces your yield to £6,000, whilst the other option, producing a gain of £8,000, allows you £5,800 tax free plus an inflation allowance in respect of capital gains. So you would pay tax on less than £2,200 ending up with a much better overall return - always providing that your total capital gains tax allowance for the year is available.

Again, when it comes to selling, there is a matter of the capital gains allowance. This could be very useful if it is not used up for the year in question and therefore adds a 'bonus' when you sell.

There are tax privileges, too, attached to certain types of investment, for example pensions and mortgages. With personal pension schemes current tax relief can save up to 40% of the cost, whilst – to the £30,000 level – your mortgage also attracts tax relief. From 6 April 1994 this will attract relief of 20%, reducing to 15% from 6 April 1995.

The taxes

Taxes which will most probably affect you when you are considering selling (or buying) savings and investment are as follows.

Income tax

You will have to pay income tax on your investment income. However, some types of investment are tax free. These include several National Savings products including National Savings Certificates, TESSAs, income from equity investments in a personal equity plan (PEP) which qualifies (see Part 3 for details).

Some investment income is untaxed when you get it, but you will still have to pay tax on it. This includes some National Savings products and Government Stocks, depending on where you bought them (see Part 3 for details).

Most investment income is paid to you with basic rate tax deducted. You will have to pay more tax if you are a higher rate tax-payer. If your income is too low for you to pay tax you should be able to reclaim any tax deducted. Examples of these types of income are: share dividends, unit trust distributions, interest on certain British Government Stocks, part of the income from purchased life annuities, income from a will which is paid out to you before the details of who gets what have been completed (see Part 3 for details).

Capital gains tax

Capital gains tax (CGT) is payable when you have disposed of chargeable assets, when you have stopped owning them. This does not include your main house or jewellery, but second homes and other possessions, such as stocks, shares, unit trusts etc. do qualify for CGT.

Establishing the level of the capital gain means working out the final value of the asset when you sold it. You then need to deduct what you paid for it and any allowable expenses incurred when the asset was in your possession (for example, improving it) or in its disposal (for example, costs of any advertising). The tax bill is also reduced (and can even be eliminated) through indexation allowances which let you avoid being taxed on gains due to inflation.

Capital gains tax applies on qualifying assets at their value on 31 March 1982 or the price of acquisition if later.

Capital gains are looked at as an extension to your income and, in general terms, the same income tax levels apply. So, if you pay basic rate tax at 25 per cent, this will be the level at which you will pay CGT until you have moved into the higher rate tax band, and then you will pay higher rate tax on the excess.

Tax-free gains

There are many exemptions to CGT. The main tax-free gains are.

- your home;
- your car;
- British Government Stocks;
- gifts to charities;
- proceeds from life insurance policies (unless you have bought the policy of a previous holder);
- winnings on the pools, the race-track etc.

In the 1993/4 tax year your first £5,800 of capital gains are tax-free, after allowing for indexation.

Inheritance tax

Inheritance tax is a tax on the total value of what you leave to others when you die. It also applies to some gifts you may make during your lifetime, if you die within seven years of making the gift.

Naturally, some gifts made are tax free, for example gifts between husband and wife. This means if you leave your house to your spouse (or vice versa) in your will, no tax is payable. Gifts made to UK charities are also tax free, as are gifts to political parties! You can also give property and possessions of outstanding national interest tax free if the gift is to a non profit-making organisation. Gifts of shares to a charitable trust can also be tax free in certain circumstances.

Inheritance tax and small businesses

Most government Budgets over the past few years have recognised the need to help small businesses by reducing the impact of inheritance tax on the transfer of interests in these organisations.

In respect of sales of disposals on or after 10 March 1992 inheritance tax is abolished on interests in unincorporated businesses; holdings above 25 per cent in unquoted and unlisted securities market companies; owner-occupied farmlands and farm tenancies. A 50 per cent relief is available for controlling holdings in fully quoted companies; certain assets owned by partnerships; and interests of landlords in let farmland.

If you are in a small business it is important for you to consult professional advisers when considering inheritance tax implications because the legislation is complex.

Finally, it is most important, when considering saving and investment generally, and particularly when you may be considering selling these, to ensure you know your tax position and whether or not the options you are considering are tax effective for you. Good timing can add to your resources, while getting the timing wrong can erode them!

CHAPTER 12

If Things Go Wrong

It is hardly ever an ideal world. Things do go wrong. Often. Sometimes seriously. It is foolish not to recognise this simple fact of life and to try to avoid it happening to you. Prevention is often much more simple than cure. It just takes that much extra effort and time to anticipate the problems which may arise. But sometimes, even when you have done everything you can to avoid trouble, it still strikes. So, what do you do when things go wrong, and where can you go for help, advice and redress? This chapter addresses these issues.

How to find out if you are in trouble

Nobody else can really give you the first alert to the fact that you could be in trouble with your savings and investments. It is up to you to be sure you have your own early warning system in place and in your consciousness, so that you can recognise the first signs of danger. Others can comment when asked, but you are really the first person who could be aware that there might be a problem that needs to be examined. So do recognise this fact.

What should you be looking for?

As has been said elsewhere in this book, you should set as an objective the fact that you wish to start each new year better off, and at least no worse off, than the preceding year. A convenient yardstick is to try to improve on the current rate of inflation by an acceptable margin. This may seem a difficult objective to achieve, but it is very worth while striving to attain. Then, if you are following the advice in this book, and reviewing where you stand at least quarterly and hopefully monthly, things should not have got too far out of hand before the alarm bells have started ringing.

Now it is time to establish the nature and the extent of the damage (loss of money, perhaps, or disappointing performance of investments), and just how serious this has been, and to take a pragmatic and realistic look at what the future can hold. Here any advisers you have may be able to help you, unless they have been giving advice about which you are now concerned. But you should recognise that the fundamental responsibility and decisions are yours, and generally yours alone.

You need to determine the following.

1. What is the extent of the erosion of your money?

2. Whose fault is it?

- Yours (perhaps through poor decision-making)?

- The economic climate (check whether your loss is greater than the norm – in which case you need to look more deeply for the reason)?

- Bad advice from your adviser which you followed (for this to be established you need to have as much of your paper-work covering the advice as possible)?

- Bad administration, from your adviser or the insurance company or other product provider (in this case you should also ensure you have the necessary paperwork to prove your point)?

- Fraud and/or incompetence (in this case you will have to establish the fact and could get help to compensate you for your loss in part at least)?

In today's financial services industry there is much help available for you if you have reasonable cause for concern in relation to those who acted for you and/or in whom you have invested your money. The compensation scheme put in place as a result of the Financial Services Act 1986 can pay you up to £48,000: 100 per cent compensation for the first £30,000 loss; and 90 per cent of the next £20,000, more details of which you will find later on in this chapter.

What you have to recognise very clearly, however, is that it is in the nature of the investment business for values to go down as well as up. If your loss is as a result of the fluctuation of markets which moved against you, you are among all those others who have also lost out, and you can't expect the industry, concerned to protect its reputation, to pay you out for taking a reasonable risk which you agreed to take at the time.

What are your rights if you feel you have lost out?

The Financial Services Act 1986 added a layer of protection which is useful in terms of protecting you from fraud or bad advice from the stray sharks in the seas of investment. It is perhaps true to say that today there may be fewer sharks around, but most of those that still exist prey on the unwary, the too-believing, and those who don't want to give adequate time and care to the choice of their investments.

There are other Acts of Parliament, too, which help to protect you. These include the Banking Act (which, among other things, guarantees 75 per cent of the first £20,000 of your deposit if the bank goes under), and the Policyholders' Protection Act which protects and guarantees 90 per cent of your entitlement if you have a long-term life insurance policy. Building societies also pay up to a maximum of £18,000 compensation, while the solicitors' scheme is still unlimited as to amount.

Since the Financial Services Act has been in force statutory powers to authorise and regulate investments have been delegated by the Department of Trade and Industry to the Securities and Investments Board (SIB). SIB in turn has recognised four other organisations, called self-regulating organisations

(SROs), to handle the detail of the work of regulation. These organisations are the Investment Management Regulatory Organisation (IMRO), largely concerned with regulating the investment management function; the Life Assurance and Unit Trust Regulatory Organisation (LAUTRO), regulating the marketing of life insurance and unit trusts; the Financial Intermediaries Managers and Brokers Regulatory Association (FIMBRA), which regulates most independent financial advisers; and the Securities and Futures Authority (SFA) which covers stockbrokers and securities dealers, and also now includes the Association of Futures Brokers and Dealers. It is now a criminal offence for anyone to carry on an investment business without authorisation from either SIB or the appropriate SRO, unless they are covered by their professional body. There are a number of Recognised Professional Bodies (RPBs), which include the chartered accountants and the solicitors whose members handle some investment business. At the time of writing it is considered that a new retail regulator, the Personal Investment Authority, will be up and running by mid 1994. This will deal with private investors and will take over the responsibilities of LAUTRO and FIMBRA who will disappear by, say, mid 1995.

Under the provisions of the Act all businesses dealing with and/or giving advice on investment must be authorised for this purpose. The process of authorisation involves their having to demonstrate to their regulator that they are being properly run, have adequate financial resources and are complying with the detailed checks and balances required under the Act. Increasingly, the spotlight is being put on the training and competence of all individuals involved in the advice-giving process, so as time goes on this should offer you increasing reassurance that your adviser is properly qualified and trained in the detailed procedures and functions of giving you competent advice.

Authorisation is given either by the SIB itself to those firms it directly regulates, or by the relevant SRO or RPB. What is vital is for you to check that the organisation you are dealing with has the necessary authorisation for the type of product being recommended to you for purchase. You can do this easily by making one simple phone call to the SIB (071-929 3652). The SIB operates a Central Register on Prestel and you will be told very quickly whether or not your adviser is authorised. You can also contact the relevant SRO or RPB for this information (see the list of names and addresses of these organisations in the Appendix).

The regulators of the industry check up all the time on the firms they are regulating. They are involved in a series of 'compliance visits' where they go through the fine detail of the member organisation's administration, records, financial audits and other relevant matters. If the regulator's compliance officer finds that matters are not what they should be the firm can be disciplined and, at worst, their authorisation removed. This is always given full publicity cover by some regulators (e.g. FIMBRA) and often given publicity cover by others and, sometimes, fines are imposed on the offenders. The use of the publicity sanction, in turn, means that you and other investors are warned that a rotten apple has been found in the barrel and removed!

The selling process

In order to determine your rights it is important to understand the selling process and how the Financial Services Act implements this.

Under the Act the basic principles are:

- that the organisation you are dealing with is supposed to offer you the best and most suitable advice in relation to the recommendations they make to suit your circumstances – known in the business as the 'best advice' rules;

- that the organisation you are dealing with operates their business on your behalf efficiently and effectively, trying to secure for you the best terms available – this is called 'best execution';

- that the organisation you are dealing with is able to ensure that you are made aware of the level of risk you are being asked to take and are comfortable with it, and that it knows all that it needs to know about you before offering advice – called the 'know your customer' rules.

In other sections of this book your attention will have been drawn to the differences between independent and tied advice. What it is important to recognise in this section is that both the independent advisers and the company representatives or tied agents have the same responsibilities as far as the range of products and services the company they are tied to provides. In either case, if nothing suits your needs, you *should* be told. However, a tied agent promoting a suitable product from his or her company's product range is not required to advise you that better products may be available from competitor companies – so you should still look around yourself.

At the beginning of the selling process both independent advisers and tied agents should have given you a leaflet called the 'Buyer's Guide', which made it clear to you whether their status was independent or tied. Independent financial advisers should also make it clear if they are paid on a commission basis (from the company whose products you may be buying) or a fee basis (by you). You'll be told by a life company the amount of commission paid to an independent adviser when they send you product particulars (but this will be after you have made your investment, although it should be within the cooling-off period when you can still cancel it). From the end of 1994, however, the position radically changes. After this it is anticipated that you will be told, in cash terms, the commission your adviser earns from the product recommended to you. You should also learn more about surrender values and real numbers in projecting future returns. These moves should curtail the current practice of selling high-cost, poor advice products.

In addition, your adviser is required to complete a Fact Find about you – this is a questionnaire which details your financial situation and on which his or her advice will be based (see Chapter 6). If you can, ensure you have a copy of this for your reference. It is a detailed process, so it should take up to an hour to be completed. If it doesn't this is not a good sign!

It is very important for any adviser you have to be sure that he or she has all the information they need before they can advise you and before you take a decision. The Act certainly tries to ensure this is the case, although it has to be said that sometimes the process is not properly carried out – it's simply used to sell!

In most cases, too, you will receive a written agreement detailing the services being provided and their cost, setting out your investment objectives and the responsibility of the adviser. However, this is less likely when you are simply buying packaged products such as life assurance or unit trusts.

The Act also ensures that proper arrangements are made for keeping your money safe before it goes into the specific investment you have chosen and this must be separate from the operating funds in the adviser's organisation. However, life being what it is, there are occasions when a con-man or woman will run away with your money and you will find that it has not been put into the investment you selected. In this case the compensation rules are brought into play, and you could find yourself recompensed by the Investors' Compensation Scheme, details of which appear below.

The promises made to you by your adviser are also dealt with under the Act. Whether these promises are given through the use of display or television advertising, in promotional literature, direct mail or in letters, the claims made, illustrations of benefits – whether in written or graph form – have to comply with rules about comparisons, reference to past performance and include any relevant risk warnings, such as 'The price of units can go down as well as up'.

Compensation

The Investors' Compensation Scheme is there to help if you lose money because your adviser has gone bust or has turned out to be a con-man or woman. The scheme is financed by the organisations who have been authorised to handle investment business. Separate schemes are in place for your protection in relation to money deposited with banks or building societies, but, as you will see from earlier chapters in this book, compensation levels are lower than for investments.

If you are in the unhappy position of dealing with an adviser whose service has failed, leading to investment losses by you,

you should hear from the Investors' Compensation Scheme, and you should certainly contact them if you feel that you could be in this position. You will find their address and phone number in the Appendix. Remember that you should have proof of any investments made, the amounts involved and as much relevant paperwork as possible. As mentioned before, the scheme can pay up to £48,000 – which provides full protection for the first £30,000 lost and 90 per cent protection for the following £20,000. There are, however, other voluntary schemes, for example the Insurance Ombudsman Bureau to which most insurance companies belong and which is the complaints handler for LAUTRO members in that scheme, which may pay more. The Insurance Ombudsman can make an award, if the case is found in your favour, of up to £100,000, which binds the member company. The Ombudsman can make a non binding recommendation for more, and there have been cases where the insurance company concerned has accepted the Ombudsman's recommendation and paid substantially more than £100,000 to the complainant. By mid 1994, when the new regulator, the Personal Investment Authority, is operational, there will be another Ombudsman Scheme introduced. The PIA Ombudsman will be concerned with complaints relating to dealings with any member of PIA.

Don't forget, too, that you have the right to sue a company for damages if you feel that the company has broken the rules of its regulator and as a result you have lost your money or lost out in other ways.

Whose responsibility is it to help and how?

So, if you feel you have a grievance, or want to complain, how do you set about it? Whose responsibility is it to try to help you and how?

The Financial Services Act has tried to ensure that there is practical help available if you, as an investor, consider you have a complaint against an authorised organisation.

All authorised businesses must have a complaints procedure. You should first put your complaint in writing to the company, at senior level, giving details and evidence of the complaint in question.

Getting the right response to your complaint is based on several points, including the way you handle making your complaint. Here are some tips to remember.

- Make your complaint to the company first of all. State the nature of the complaint clearly and succinctly, with only necessary and sufficient points, and avoiding any details that, however annoying they may be to you, are sidelines to the main issue involved. Ensure that you identify what you want the company to do about the complaint and set a time limit for their response.

- Enclose as much documentation as you can with your initial letter of complaint (copies and not originals).

- Make a note of any telephone calls and/or other conversations relevant to the complaint.

- If you don't get the complaint resolved, take it to a higher authority within the company – preferably the chief executive, having taken the trouble to find out the exact name and address.

- If you still find the complaint unresolved, find out whether the company is in membership of an Ombudsman scheme, and which regulatory body has authorised it.

- Write to the appropriate regulatory body or Ombudsman, giving them the background to the complaint and telling them of your previous approaches to the company which have resulted in either no action or unsatisfactory responses. Remember that the letterhead, visiting card etc. of the organisation you are dealing with should identify the regulator. The regulator will have a system set up to deal with your complaint. Systems vary within regulators, but all have a number of ways in which your complaint can be dealt with if they find that rules have been broken. As a result you may receive payment or compensation for any loss or distress you have been caused.

- Do remember that all this takes time . . .

- If you are told by the regulatory body or the Ombudsman that you do not have a case, believe it! Don't spend good time and money progressing a matter which is unlikely to end in a satisfactory outcome for you. The procedures which are now in place to give you satisfaction if you have a good case have been thought through in detail and they work – in your interests.

Finally, do remember that if it is just a case of losing money because of the ups and downs in the market, this is considered as a normal investment risk and won't qualify you for compensation!

If, however, you have been dealing with an unauthorised firm (which would have been acting illegally in this case), you should get in touch with the SIB to let them know the position. It is their responsibility to try to ensure that unauthorised firms are not allowed to operate and they should act swiftly to ensure this.

In addition to the regulators (SIB, the SROs and the RPBs), there are several sector trade associations which help with complaints. The names and addresses of some of the key financial trade associations are included in the Appendix of this book. The sector trade press (identified in the Appendix) will also be helpful with your question or enquiry.

It is important to realise, with regard to the subject of complaints in general, that while all the regulators are still operating under different systems with differing terms and conditions, the intention is to try to make the system easier and more consistent for the consumer in trouble. In the future it is hoped that there will be 'one-stop shopping' for the consumer with a problem, and that you won't be shunted around. In the meantime, however, the regulators do appreciate the problems faced by consumers, and so, if you approach the wrong regulator for your purpose, you should find that you are helped to identify the right one, and you should find that you get a warm, helpful response to your enquiry.

PART THREE

POPULAR OPTIONS FOR YOUR MONEY

The financial services industry is a market-place with many products and services on offer. These are often given 'brand names' by the individual companies in each sector. As a result, as a potential customer, you may find it all very confusing, especially as it is virtually impossible to compare like with like. Each product is naturally portrayed as more attractive than its competitor!

This part of the book seeks to simplify and sort out the market-place for you. Clearly it cannot cover all the options on offer, but it will include the most popular. It will aim to tell you, in clear and direct language, the benefits which a particular family of products may have to offer – for example, unit trusts. It will also spell out potential difficulties and drawbacks which you may experience.

As a result you should find that you may not need to study *all* the material in this section of the book – you can easily refer to the areas in which you are particularly interested.

This part is divided into three main headings.

- **Green for go – the 'safety first' options** These are especially suitable for you if you want maximum security, combined with a low level of risk. In this case, you should understand that your opportunities for financial gain will be more limited.

- **Amber for the 'each way' bet** These are for you if you want to be in the middle of the road, with a chance of a reasonable gain, but with some assurances of safety for your money.

- **Red for 'alert'** These are for you if you are happy to surrender varying degrees of security in order to have the maximum opportunities for financial gain. These options contain the most risk and so should present you with opportunities to win the most reward, but remember – nothing is ever certain in the world of investment.

In practice, those with a large amount of savings may be best advised to invest in all three – green, amber and red – to spread the load.

By way of introduction, you must think first about what is

important for you. Ensuring you can make ends meet, have sufficient life insurance and are on your way to a reasonable retirement and pension are all essential to providing good money management.

Next, you need to decide whether your requirement is to save regularly, and whether or not you may have a need to withdraw (occasionally or in an emergency). Alternatively, your savings and investments may be directed towards a specific objective, e.g. to buy a house or to afford that holiday of a lifetime. Ultimately, you will need to be sure that any lump sum investment you have made is prudent, also that you have borne in mind your long-term priorities. In terms of time, this may be way ahead now, but some day it will be tomorrow. You need to be sure that your mature years can be economically comfortable and stress-free, also that those who are near and dear to you can be considered before you are beyond taking the right decisions in their future interests!

Parts 1 and 2 of this book should help you to consider your position with regard to the above matters. Then you should be able to judge which of the options set out below are worth researching further in order to meet specific priorities you have identified as important.

Green for Go – the Safety-First Options

Before you consider the options set out below, bear in mind the impact of inflation if you are intending to put all your long-term savings money into 'Green for Go' investments. Over the last twenty years those who might have done this would have experienced the ravaging of their capital because of the high rate of inflation at the time! At the time of writing inflation is low, under 4 per cent, but things do have a habit of changing, so be on your guard.

Fixed capital, fixed interest

These are the safest of all investments. You know exactly where you stand, at all times. Here are some examples of this type of investment.

BANK

'Term' accounts

These are lump sum, fixed interest rate investment accounts. Your money can be tied up for periods varying from one month to five years. You don't necessarily get more interest if you opt for the longer term. They are suitable for everyone (especially at a time of relatively high interest rates) who takes a view that interest rates may fall and wants to protect themselves against that eventuality. Be careful, though, to recognise your loss of flexibility. There is normally a minimum investment, usually £2,000, but upper limits go to sums in excess of £250,000. Naturally interest rates vary according to the sum invested. There are no charges. Interest is paid net of basic rate tax at the lower levels and gross at the higher levels of investment.

Your investor protection comes from the bank compensation scheme, covering 75 per cent of your savings up to £20,000.

Buying and Selling: Through the bank of your choice.

Upside: You know where you stand at all times.

Downside: Your money has less opportunity to 'grow' as it could do if you took more risk. Not suitable for those who pay no tax, e.g. children.

Money market
Banks offer money market accounts in many combinations of the notice and fixed interest accounts. Generally these relate to sums below £100,000.

Flexibility is provided by notice accounts with periods starting with instant access, seven days, fourteen days, one, three and six months' notice. Minimum deposit is likely to be £50,000 for instant access and £10,000 for other periods. Rates of interest vary in relation to market rates and interest is paid half-yearly.

Fixed accounts set the rate of interest at the outset and this remains stable throughout the period of the deposit: minimum is seven days and maximum five years. Interest is paid when the deposit matures or, if your deposit is for a term longer than one year, on the anniversary of the account being opened. If your money is on deposit for more than six months you may be able to elect to have interest paid monthly.

Minimum deposit varies with the term. Up to one month it is £50,000, from one to six months £25,000, and for six months and over £5,000.

Your investor protection comes from the bank compensation scheme, covering 75 per cent of your savings up to £20,000.

Buying and Selling: Through the bank of your choice.

Upside: A useful option for those with money.

Downside: If you are looking for the long-term benefit you should consider other equity-based options before you take a decision.

TESSAs

TESSAs are the relatively new tax-exempt special savings accounts. They are five-year accounts for either regular or lump sum savings. In order to qualify for the tax-free interest you have to leave the money in for the full five years. If you withdraw the interest before the five years are up, it will be paid to you net of basic rate tax, but you will have to wait for the end of the five-year term to qualify for the relevant amount of tax-free bonus. Also, if you withdraw your money before the end of the term the interest is taxable. These accounts are suitable for those who can make lump sum deposits from time to time, recognising that their money will be 'locked away' for five years, and in this respect they are especially attractive for higher rate tax-payers. There is an overall maximum investment over five years, currently £9,000. The maximum amount which can be saved regularly is £150 a month. Maximum lump sums are currently £3,000 in year one, £1,800 in years two to four, and £600 in year five. There are no charges.

Buying and Selling: Through your bank, building society or financial adviser.

Upside: One of the most secure ways of getting a good return with very little risk – and tax free if held for the full five-year term.

Downside: What happens if you really need the money in the interim? You could lose the very attractive tax advantages. On balance, though, a good option for taxpayers to consider.

INSURANCE

Guaranteed growth and income bonds

These are lump sum investments with fixed returns over terms ranging from one to five years and sometimes more. If you are paid interest each year it is an 'income bond'; if the interest is left to accumulate it is called a 'growth bond'. These investments are suitable for anyone over the specified minimum age (sixteen or eighteen, depending on the terms of the particular contract), but especially for those looking to increase their income at retirement or those trying to build up a nest egg before they retire. There are charges, of course, and these are built into the overall terms. Interest is paid net of basic rate tax. However, you could lose out if you surrender your bond before its maturity date.

Your investor protection comes from the policy-holders' protection scheme, covering 90 per cent of the benefits agreed. But if you choose a bond from an overseas insurance company, you will be at risk because you will not be covered by the protection scheme against loss.

Buying and Selling: Through your financial adviser, insurance broker, or bank or building society.

Upside: In general terms you tend to get a good competitive return for your money.

Downside: If you need to cash in early you may lose out heavily. Check the small print carefully and make sure the insurance company you select is covered by the policy-holders' protection scheme.

Annuities

These are lump sum investments on which you can't change your mind once your decision is taken and the money is handed over! In return for your money you will receive an income for life. The amount you will receive is dependent on many factors, including your age, the lump sum involved etc. In general terms the older you are the more you will get because, naturally, the term for paying out will be shorter! The amount you will get is normally fixed from the beginning of the contract, and is also dependent on interest rates, although you should be able to choose the terms of the contract to provide an income which continues until the surviving spouse dies, or a guaranteed income which will continue for a set period, say five to ten years, regardless of whether you survive yourself. While the option is open to everyone, it is most attractive to those over seventy years of age. The charges are built into the contract terms. The annual payment you receive has basic rate tax deducted at source.

Your investor protection is through the policy-holders' protection scheme (UK providers only) and covers 90 per cent of the benefits.

Buying and Selling: Through your financial adviser, insurance broker, bank or building society.

Upside: A trouble-free option of exchanging some of your capital for an agreed income. It is particularly attractive for the elderly, hopefully providing a release from worry and administration work.

Downside: It is strictly a 'one-way street'. If your circumstances change you won't be able to get at your money!

LOCAL AUTHORITY

Fixed term loans

These are lump sum investments paying a fixed rate of interest over set periods (one to ten years). They are suitable for those who can and want to set aside savings for a given period and are open to anyone who is nineteen or over. The schemes of the different authorities vary in relation to minimum investments. Some can be as low as £100, while others require minimum sums of up to £1,000. There are no charges and, of course, no withdrawal is possible until the end of the term. Interest is paid usually half-yearly, net of basic rate tax.

Do remember that some local authorities are a better buy than others.

Buying and Selling: Through the local authority of your choice (the treasurer's department) or by filling in a coupon in their advertisement in the newspaper.

Upside: A good and trouble-free option.

Downside: You can't change your mind, you are locked in and could face difficulty if your circumstances change.

Yearling bonds

These are lump sum investments paying fixed rate interest for the one-year period. You can buy these investments on the Stock Exchange, as a collection of loans from a selection of local authorities. Sometimes the bonds are issued at a small discount to the nominal value. They are suitable for those looking for short-term, fixed interest investments and open to anyone aged eighteen or over. There are no charges and minimum investment is £1,000. If you want to get the best from this type of investment you should hold it to maturity, but you can sell earlier if you want to. Basic rate tax is deducted at source. If you sell at a profit it will be considered a capital gain and will be subject to capital gains tax assessment.

Buying and Selling: Through a bank share-dealing service or a stockbroker.

Upside: A good option for those seeking a competitive return.

Downside: You could lose some of the benefits if you sell early.

NATIONAL SAVINGS

Capital bonds

These are lump sum investments similar to National Savings certificates although, unlike savings certificates, interest is paid gross, but is subject to tax if you are a tax-payer. The interest is

137

calculated daily but only added annually. Capital bonds are designed as five-year investments, so it pays to consider them as such. They are for everyone and there is a minimum value of £100. No charges apply and you can withdraw your money in full or part in multiples of £100, providing you leave a balance of £100 in the bond.

Buying and Selling: Through forms available at your local post office.

Upside: A good and safe option for most people. But check the current rate of return at your local post office.

Downside: You are assessed for income tax annually on the interest accumulating in the capital bond, even though you can't actually receive your interest until the five-year term is up!

National Savings certificates

There are a number of types of these lump sum investments, including an index-linked certificate, which keeps up with the current levels of inflation. These latter were better known under the name of 'Granny bonds'. Index-linked certificates are suitable for small to medium-sized amounts which can then grow in line with increases in the cost of living as measured by the retail prices index. You have to hold the certificates for twelve months to earn the index-linked benefits. You can check up on the value of your 'Granny bonds' in the press or at post offices. The final compound bonus can be an attractive feature of this option for savings. This is a good, tax-free investment for top-rate tax-payers.

National Savings certificates are also available in a fixed rate form. They are suitable for small amounts which should be held for five years to obtain the maximum benefits which are tax free. You can make earlier withdrawals if you have to. National Savings certificates, both index linked and fixed rate are particularly attractive to higher rate tax-payers. The minimum is £25 (one unit) and there is currently a maximum of £10,000. No charges are made. Interest earned is tax free and you have no need to declare this on your tax return.

National Savings certificates are suitable for everyone and, in particular, as gifts for children and others.

Buying and Selling: Through forms available at your local post office.

Upside: An option everyone should consider, safe and attractive, particularly to higher rate tax-payers. The index-linked version is especially attractive if you believe that inflation is bound to increase in the future.

Downside: You need to leave your money in for the full five years to gain the maximum interest because the rate of interest is low in the first two to three years.

Yearly plans

These are monthly savings plans for regular savers for one year giving a fixed rate of interest. You can then arrange for your plan to be held for a further four years to earn a higher fixed rate of interest. The scheme also provides for the plan-holder to take out a subsequent plan for a further twelve monthly payments. Interest is reinvested and tax free. These are suitable for those who wish to invest regularly. They are suitable for everyone and the minimum monthly payment is £20 in multiples of £5, and a maximum of £400. There are no charges and if you want to withdraw money you will need to give fourteen days' notice, but the only permissible units of payment are either all the payments so far made or whole certificates with accrued interest. The interest rates quoted when you start your yearly plan apply for the full five years. You will get a lower rate if you cash in your plan earlier. Interest is free of tax and you need not declare this on your tax return.

Buying and Selling: Through forms available at your local post office.

Upside: A good option, suitable for those who wish to save monthly and receive a tax-free return on their savings.

Downside: Difficult to see any minus points, but you need to watch your timing to get the best interest returns.

As in the case of all options from National Savings, your investor protection is the guarantee provided by the government.

Fixed capital, variable interest

BANK

Deposit accounts

These are interest-bearing accounts which require seven days' notice to withdraw your money. You will lose seven days' interest if you insist on immediate withdrawal. They are suitable for everyone and you can open an account with a £1 minimum deposit. Interest is variable, usually paid half-yearly, net of basic rate tax, unless you are a non tax-payer in which case you can ask, on Form R85, for your interest to be paid to you gross. (It is as well to remember that many people can elect to have bank/building society interest paid gross, so ask if you want to try to achieve this.)

Your investor protection comes from the bank savings compensation scheme, covering 75 per cent of your savings up to £20,000.

Buying and Selling: Through your local bank branch.

Upside: A useful option, offering flexibility.

Downside: You can get a better return for your money if you can manage your finances well.

Children's account

These are bank accounts designed to appeal to children, who are offered free gifts, magazines and useful services to encourage them to understand the use of a bank account. In general terms they are targeted at children under sixteen and, in due course, they are exchanged for the other traditional bank accounts. Minimum amount to open an account is £1 to £10. Interest is variable. Withdrawal without giving seven days' notice can result in loss of interest for those seven days. Signature of the parent is required for withdrawal by a child under the age of seven.

(A point to be aware of is that there is a trend, innovated by the Trustee Savings Bank to encourage 'Family' accounts. These pay higher rates of interest for a group of 'family deposit/ savings accounts'.)

Investor protection is under the bank compensation scheme, covering 75 per cent of savings up to £20,000.

Buying and Selling: Your local bank branch.

Upside: A useful option to persuade children it is in their interest to learn money management early. It gives them a useful return on their money.

Downside: It needs time to supervise and manage on behalf of the child.

High interest cheque accounts

These are interest-bearing current accounts. There is a minimum investment of usually some £2,000. You will get a cheque book, and could have standing order, credit card and overdraft facilities. They are suitable for people aged eighteen or over. Interest is variable, and normally not much higher than the standard deposit accounts, calculated daily, but you will need to keep your minimum balance in the account if you don't want the interest rate to drop sharply! Interest is paid net of basic rate tax, unless you are a non tax-payer, in which case you can ask, on Form R85, for your interest to be paid to you gross.

Your investor protection comes from the bank compensation scheme, covering 75 per cent of your savings up to £20,000.

Buying and Selling: Your local bank branch.

Upside: You get a little more interest on your account.

Downside: You could do better if you can manage money well – not really suitable as a means of savings.

Monthly savings accounts (Save-as-you-earn)

These accounts are designed to help those who intend to save regularly. You can vary your level of savings after six months and you can miss one month's savings. If you cease to save regularly the account will become a traditional deposit account. The accounts are suitable for anyone and the minimum saved can be as low as £10 a month. There are no charges and there is a limited withdrawal facility. Interest is variable and is paid net of basic rate tax.

Your investor protection is through the bank compensation scheme, covering 75 per cent of savings up to £20,000.

Buying and Selling: Through your local bank branch.

Upside: A useful tool to help you towards better money management.

Downside: You could do better if you are prepared to make the effort!

Notice account

These accounts are designed to be attractive to those with lump sums available. They require one, two, three or six months' notice to withdraw funds, but you do have the option of losing interest if you want to make an immediate withdrawal. They are open to everyone, but are particularly attractive to those with sums from £100 to £50,000 able to take advantage of the interest 'steps' available in this competitive market-place. Interest rates are variable and interest is paid net of basic rate tax.

Your investor protection is through the bank compensation scheme, covering 75 per cent of your savings up to £20,000.

Buying and Selling: Through the bank of your choice.

Upside: You get a competitive return for your money.

Downside: Your money does not have the chance to 'grow' in terms of getting the level of capital appreciation if you had it invested in the equity markets in the long term.

NATIONAL SAVINGS

Income bonds
These are lump sum investments paying interest monthly without deduction of tax at source. The level of interest paid will vary, but usually income bonds remain competitive. There should be fewer changes to the level of interest than on bank options. Income bonds are particularly suitable for retired people, although the variable interest rates make it difficult to budget. They are suitable for everyone. Minimum investment is £2,000 (in multiples of £1,000) and maximum is £250,000. No charges are made. If you want to withdraw you must also do this in multiples of £1,000, providing you leave the minimum £2,000 in the bond. You are required to give three months' notice of withdrawal. Interest is paid gross, on the fifth day of the month, to your specified bank or other institution.

Buying and Selling: Through forms available at your local post office.

Upside: A good option for most people.

Downside: Variable interest rates are a drawback and the three months' notice required does not make this option suitable for 'emergency' money.

Investment accounts
These accounts pay fairly competitive interest rates which change less frequently than bank deposit account rates. Interest accumulates gross. They are suitable for everyone and an amount of £20 or over is required for each deposit. Maximum investment is £100,000 inclusive of interest earned on the account. No charges are made and you can withdraw your money with

one month's notice. Interest, which is variable, is normally credited to your account on 31 December each year.

Buying and Selling: Through application forms available at your local post office.

Upside: A good, safe option.

Downside: Difficult to see any minus points other than the one-month notice required means this is not suitable for 'emergency' money where instant access is needed.

Ordinary accounts

These are essentially two-tiered accounts using post office counters. They offer modest interest which is partly tax free, but you do get easy access to your money and the benefit of some banking services. They are suitable for everyone and the spread is £5 to £10,000. No charges are made, and withdrawal facilities are quick and easy to use. Interest is earned at a guaranteed 5 per cent for each month, provided the account is open for the full calendar year and you have at least £500 in the account, otherwise the interest rate is halved. You will get no interest on a month in which you make an investment or withdrawal. The first £70 of interest is tax free.

Buying and Selling: Through forms available at your local post office.

Upside: A useful option, although the rate of interest is rarely competitive.

Downside: You could do much better if you think you can handle your money well.

BUILDING SOCIETY

Cash card accounts

These accounts offer an easy-to-use system for withdrawals and deposits. They are operated through the 'hole in the wall' systems in the LINK network and are increasingly popular. They are suitable for anyone and offer many other banking services, such as standing orders and statements. The minimum required to open an account is £1 and, as with the bank cash cards, you can withdraw up to £100 to £250 daily from the ATMs (automatic teller machines) and larger amounts by cheque. Interest is variable, usually paid half-yearly, net of basic rate tax. If you are a non tax-payer you can ask, on Form R85, for your interest to be paid to you gross. There are no charges.

Your investor protection is through the building societies compensation scheme covering 90 per cent of savings up to £20,000.

Buying and Selling: Through the local branch of your selected building society.

Upside: A useful and flexible service.

Downside: You could do better if you can manage your time and money well.

Cheque book accounts

These accounts work in a similar way to a current account at the bank. You get a cheque book and a cheque guarantee card in most cases, but not all offer overdraft facilities. They are suitable for anyone of eighteen or over and the minimum amount needed to open an account is £1. Charges are generally lower than for banks. You can withdraw cash on demand by using your cheque book, up to £150 per day. Interest is variable and is sometimes scaled to give you more return if you leave larger sums in the account. Interest is paid net of basic rate tax, unless you are a non tax-payer, in which case you can ask, on Form R85, for your interest to be paid to you gross.

Your investor protection is via the building societies compensation scheme, covering 90 per cent of savings up to £20,000.

Buying and Selling: Through the local branch of your building society.

Upside: A useful and flexible service.

Downside: You could do better if you can manage your time and money well.

Children's account

These accounts are designed to appeal to children, much in the same way as children's bank accounts. They were provided in response to research which suggested that the younger a child gets the banking or saving habit, the more unlikely it will be that they will take the decision to change to another source of supply when they are adults! As a result, many incentives are put on offer to tempt the young customer. These can range from gifts of many sorts to money boxes which have a more direct connection with the financial services industry. Junior customers may also have the added advantage of beneficial interest rates. These accounts are suitable for children of different ages, usually grouped as under and over eleven, and targeted with different incentives accordingly. The minimum to open an account is £1 and there are no charges applied. Withdrawals are as per the accounts for adults, to £250 cash per day. Parents' signatures will be required for withdrawals if the child is under seven and occasionally if the sum is large until the child reaches ten or twelve. Interest is variable and there are wide variations in rates. As minors are considered to be non tax-payers the interest will be paid gross, but the parents have the responsibility to register the child as a non tax-payer. Interest is paid either annually or half-yearly.

Investor protection is through the building societies compensation scheme, covering 90 per cent of savings up to the £20,000 maximum.

Buying and Selling: Through the local branch of your building society.

Upside: A useful service to encourage children to manage their money well.

Downside: Parents need to spend time to inaugurate and supervise, in the interests of the child.

Instant access accounts

These accounts offer higher rates of interest, often based on the amounts held in the account, so the more you leave in the account the more interest you will get. They are suitable for lump sum investments, particularly for the use of money which you have got 'on hold', or pending putting it to other and better use elsewhere. These accounts are open to anyone, but there is generally a minimum deposit. This varies widely from society to society. It could be as low as £1, or it could be as high as £500 or £1,000. You can withdraw on demand from any branch, usually up to £250 a day in cash, up to £15,000 by cheque.

Your investor protection comes under the building societies compensation scheme, covering 90 per cent of savings up to a maximum of £20,000.

Buying and Selling: Through the local branch of your building society.

Upside: An attractive and competitive option which has proved useful to many during the early days of this recession.

Downside: For those who understand investment and can accept taking risks, they could do better to make their money 'grow'.

Notice accounts

These accounts are for lump sum investment and require notice periods of seven days, one, two or three months to withdraw funds. There is generally a loss of interest over a given period to accommodate you if you wish to have instant access. Accounts are planned to ensure that there is more interest for those customers who leave larger sums in the account. They are suitable for short and long-term savings, and are open to anyone. Minimums vary from society to society, but are generally in the region of £500 to £1,000. There are no charges. Interest is variable and interest periods also vary, but six-monthly and annual are most frequent. Larger investors can earn substantially more from their money, from 1 to 3 per cent. Interest is paid net of basic rate tax, unless you are a non tax-payer, in which case you can ask, on Form R85, for your interest to be paid to you gross.

Your investor protection is under the building societies compensation scheme, covering 90 per cent of savings up to a maximum of £20,000.

Buying and Selling: Through the local branch of your building society.

Upside: A useful and competitive option.

Downside: If you are prepared to take risks you are likely to do better – if you are patient and view risk investments as part of a mixed bag of savings, and hold them as long-term savings.

Share accounts
The ordinary or share accounts are the basic, familiar building society accounts. These offer easy access and very modest interest rates. In today's competitive environment there are many better options for your money. They are open to anyone, but it is likely that, as time goes by, most people will avoid them, apart, that is, as a haven for their 'emergency' money – the amount, however small, you may need to pay those unexpected bills. The minimum is £1 and the withdrawals are in common with most other building society accounts, up to £250 daily in cash, and by cheque from branches (sometimes with a maximum limit of, say, up to £5,000). Interest is variable, paid half-yearly, net of basic rate tax, unless you are a non tax-payer, in which case you can ask, on Form R85, for interest to be paid to you gross.

Your investor protection is through the building societies compensation scheme, covering 90 per cent of savings up to a maximum of £20,000.

Buying and Selling: Through the local branch of your building society.

Upside: A very safe, traditional option. Ideal for 'rainy day' money.

Downside: You could certainly do better for your money!

TESSAs

Building societies also offer tax exempt special savings accounts. See page 134 for details.

Term share

These are lump sum investments which lock away your money for a given period, from one to five years. Sometimes you can withdraw your money if you need it, but you will suffer a loss of interest by way of penalty. Interest rates are generous by building society standards. They are suitable for modest lump sum investment, providing you know you are not going to need the money, and are open to anyone. There is generally a minimum, from £500 to £1,000. Interest is usually variable, paid annually or half-yearly and sometimes monthly. Interest is paid net of basic rate tax.

Your investor protection is through the building societies compensation scheme, covering 90 per cent of savings up to £20,000.

Buying and Selling: Through the local branch of your building society.

Upside: A useful option which pays reasonably well.

Downside: A degree of inflexibility.

OFFSHORE

High interest cheque accounts

This is an interest-bearing current account. There is usually a minimum level of £1,000 or more to open an account. The account is operated at a bank or branch of a UK bank in the Channel Islands or the Isle of Man. It works very like a traditional current account, but there are often specific arrangements regarding minimum cheque withdrawals and other related banking services. You are unlikely to be allowed an overdraft facility. Charges are modest. Interest is variable, paid without deduction of tax. If you live in the UK you will have to declare interest and pay tax on the interest you receive.

There is no specific investor protection, unless you are dealing with a bank which is a subsidiary of a UK bank, and you need to check its status carefully.

Buying and Selling: You can get the address of the offshore subsidiary from your local UK bank.

Upside: You should get a higher return for your money in normal circumstances and the interest is paid gross.

Downside: You have no investor protection unless you are dealing with a subsidiary of a UK bank or company. It is vital to check this out before you take a decision so you know exactly where you stand and what level of risk you are being asked to take. As usual, beware of those companies which advertise interest rates that are well out of line with the market. The higher the rate of interest quoted, the higher the risk!

Other offshore options

These include term accounts, unit trusts and others. Refer to their other entries in this book and consider that the offshore option means you will be able to get interest paid gross, but if you are a UK resident you will have to declare it and pay tax on it. It is very important to check the investor protection you may or may not get if you go down this road.

If you are thinking of offshore options, research the offshore gilt funds which offer a high gross rate (usually well above building society rates), but remember the caveat that some of these also involve repayment of capital in order to achieve high returns. They are, however, a good and reasonably safe way of maximising income.

PENSIONS

Additional voluntary contributions (AVCs)
These are the additional contributions which you can pay into your tax-free regular savings plan for at least five years. These can either be linked to your company pension scheme or be free-standing. Remember that currently your pension contributions, including any AVCs, must not exceed 15 per cent of your earnings. Since October 1987 it has been possible to have your own 'free-standing' AVC, quite separate from the firm's pension scheme. They are suitable for anyone, provide a boost to your pension and are particularly attractive to higher rate tax-payers. Charges are built into the scheme. Your payments into your fund are non taxable, but the pension you receive will be considered as earned income. The commuted sum (amount from the overall fund which you can elect to have as a lump sum) is tax free.

Your investor protection is under the Policyholders' Protection Act and covers 90 per cent of benefits if you are with a UK authorised insurer. If you are with a building society you are covered by the building society compensation scheme.

Buying and Selling: Through an insurance company, a bank or a building society offering these schemes.

Upside: Good benefits are achievable and the tax position is attractive.

Downside: It is difficult to see any minus points, except that your money is 'locked in' until it is paid to you as a pension.

Amber for Each-Way Bet – Some Safety, Some Gain

This is the first stepping-stone off the safety-first ladder. You will know where you stand in relation to the interest you will earn on your money, but the capital values can fluctuate in relation to the movements in the world's money markets.

Variable capital, fixed interest

GOVERNMENT STOCK OR GILT-EDGED SECURITIES (GILTS)

These are a range of options where you can invest lump sums in the government to help fund government spending – in other words you loan your money to the government. Most of these stocks are issued with a fixed interest rate. At the end of a predetermined period the stock will be redeemed by the government at what is called the 'full nominal value' – in other words the known published amount. What you will get in return is the 'yield' or the interest paid on your money, paid half-yearly net of basic rate tax. In terms of using gilts, the yield is the important barometer of value. This should be reviewed in relation to the interest rates current at the time. If these are low, it follows that gilts with a better rate of interest will be popular but expensive. Remember that when you examine the prices of gilts in the press you will see two yields often featured. One of these is the basic yield or interest paid on your money, the other is the assessment of the net 'redemption' yield and this takes into account any capital gain or loss you would make if you held the stock to redemption. There is no official minimum, but it is usual to buy in units of £250 or more. Charges are modest, for example if you buy through a post office it costs £1 including VAT for a £250 purchase, and you can withdraw any amount at the current price if you don't want to hold your gilts to redemption date.

(A point to remember: At times of extreme economic and/or other difficulty investment in government stock can be hazardous, as those who were caught out by the old War Loan stock earlier this century will well recall!)

Buying and Selling: Through your bank, stockbroker or at the local post office.

Upside: A good, safe option when seeking a high return – can also be used for capital gain. It offers a regular income and a guaranteed return of the nominal capital if held to the redemption date.

Downside: You could do better for your money in the equity markets in good times. Values fluctuate daily and you could lose out if you want to get your money back early. When interest rates are low, many gilts will cost more than their face value to buy, resulting in a capital loss on redemption.

INSURANCE

With-profits endowment

These are frequently used for regular savings over fixed periods of ten years or more. The sum 'insured' is guaranteed and is paid out when the policy matures or on your death, if this happens before the end of the fixed term. To this sum will be added any bonuses which have been earned from the investments made by the insurance company under the policy. There are two kinds of bonuses, the annual (or reversionary) bonus – which is secure, as it cannot be withdrawn from the policy and also a final bonus (called a terminal bonus) which is paid at maturity. Both bonuses can vary in amount, depending on the performance of the investment market and the company with which you are assured. The terminal bonus has a considerable effect on the money you can receive – frequently doubling the sum paid out when compared with the surrender value in the final years of the policy, thus there are huge incentives to keep an endowment policy until maturity.

Your money, after expenses, is invested into a life fund by the insurance company; most commonly this is a mix of government stocks, property and equity shareholdings.

There have been some unfair criticisms of with-profit endowment policies recently. This is because they are all too often related to home purchase and have sometimes been the subject of mis-selling. However, they still offer many attractions if used in the right circumstances. They are open to anyone over the age of eight and the minimum payment can be as low as £5 monthly. While there are facilities to withdraw money and to stop payments, these should be examined carefully before taking a decision, as early cashing in of the policy or turning it into a 'paid-up' policy (where no further payments are made and the policy is paid out at maturity in relation to the payments you have made) could cost you dearly! If you do have an urgent need to cash your policy in, take the trouble to research what you may get if you sold on the open market, as it is likely that you could get better terms than your insurance company would pay you. For example, if you surrender early (in the first five years) you are unlikely to receive back an amount equal to the money you have paid in; conversely a policy held until maturity can provide you with a handsome tax-free lump sum. The charges are built into the contract. Interest is variable and is built into the bonus system.

Your investor protection comes through two routes: the first is the Policyholders' Protection Act which covers 90 per cent of the benefits, the second (if the insurance company is a member and the vast majority are) through the Insurance Ombudsman Bureau if a complaint you make is upheld.

Buying and Selling: Through an insurance broker or financial adviser, alternatively through the company of your choice direct.

Upside: Past results have indicated that, in the right circumstances, endowment assurance has provided a good return for your money.

Downside: Times are changing – you need to go into the fine print with the company/adviser of your choice to ensure you know what it is reasonable for you to expect from endowment assurance in the future. Remember that it is likely you will have to pay high up-front charges which could be 80 per cent of the first year's premium. It may be possible for you to negotiate this point with your adviser, so try it!

Personal pension plans

From July 1988 you have been free to save for your own pension through a personal pension plan. You have also been free to opt out of your company pension scheme into your own personal pension plan, if that is your wish. Your employer too, has the option of contributing to your personal pension plan. There are some attractive benefits in doing your own thing in relation to your pension, but beware, because there are many drawbacks too ... There have been several cases of over-enthusiastic salespeople tempting people to transfer out of their company pension schemes into a personal pension plan. As a result people have lost out when a proper comparison of benefits in each is compared. Don't forget, too, that it is profitable for an adviser to try to get you to change and the commission he or she receives comes from your pocket! That is not to say that the option should not be examined. Frequently it can be very worth while, but you do need to examine all the facts in your particular case very carefully and call for confirmation of all details in writing.

Your investor protection comes under the Financial Services Act, but there are special arrangements for those obtaining personal pensions through building society deposits which are not covered under the Act.

Buying and Selling: From insurance companies, banks, building societies and financial advisers.

Upside: Good benefits can be achieved and the tax position is attractive.

Downside: You need to ensure that your technical knowledge is good and that you are being well advised, with no chance of anyone pulling the wool over your eyes.

Company loan stock and debenture stock

This is a lump sum investment whereby you loan your money to a company for a fixed interest return over a fixed period. At the end of the period your money is returned in full. In the mean time, however, the value of your loan stock may fall or rise in relation to the movements in the investment market, also the market sector in which the company trades. As with Government Stocks the 'net redemption' yield quoted takes into account assessments of capital gains or losses likely over the period, also the interest provided to you which is expressed as yield. There is often an option to convert your loan or debenture stock into ordinary shares at a date and price which is predetermined.

It is suitable for most taxpayers and is open to you if you are eighteen or over. The minimum investment to make it worth while is £1,000 or over. Charges are at the level of a stockbroker's commission. There is nothing to pay in charges on new issues nor on redemption and you can withdraw at any time, but you may receive back less than you invested.

Your investor protection is through the investors' compensation scheme, maximum £48,000.

Buying and Selling: Through a stockbroker, your bank, many building societies or a financial adviser.

Upside: Reasonable option at most times. A useful investment as part of an income-seeking portfolio.

Downside: You could probably do better for your money in good times.

Red for Alert – Greater Risk and a Chance of Greater Reward

This is the final step up the savings and investments ladder, open to all, but only to be used when you are prepared to take some risk and when you have sufficient money saved or invested in the 'Green for Go' and 'Amber' sections. The options are many and varied. Do remember, though, that both the capital value of your investment and the income you earn from it are both at risk! However, nothing ventured, nothing gained. On balance 'Red for Alert' investments should be viewed as long term – for at least five years and preferably longer.

Variable capital, variable interest

UNIT TRUSTS

These are the essential 'starter kits' for investment in equities. They are a collective investment where you put your money with the money of many other people into a professionally managed fund. This fund is then invested in the shares of companies, and can include investment in Government Stocks, proportions in cash and unlisted securities (see Glossary). All of this is determined by the trust deed which is set for each and every unit trust. It is important to remember the two benefits which unit trusts offer – the first is that your money will be professionally managed in a way which you, as an individual, would find almost impossible on a day-to-day basis, and the second is that the money itself, the fund, is held by other, independent, trustees so that the managers themselves, the unit trust company, don't have an opportunity to be tempted to help themselves to your money! You have a multiplicity of choices of investment using unit trusts. You can invest for growth or for income, or a mixture of the two; in specialist sectors; in specialist companies; particular parts of the world; and varieties of combinations of all of these.

You can invest a lump sum, usually a minimum investment of £500 to £1,000, or save regularly through a regular unit trust savings scheme for as little as £25 to £30 a month. Unit trusts can also form the basis of a PEP (see page 162). In addition, there are many unit-linked options which combine the benefits of investment in unit trusts with the stability of insurance. Then, as well, there are those unit-linked contracts which are linked to 'managed funds', i.e. funds which are unitised, and which also invest in a mix of gilts, money, property and equities.

Unit trusts are ideally suited to first-time investors who don't mind taking some risks: for savings on behalf of children, also for those of mature years who want to ensure the possibility of greater income tomorrow through sacrificing higher income today. They are suitable for anyone, at all but the most modest of income/investment levels. Charges are at two levels: an initial charge when you buy and an annual maintenance charge. You can check up on the price of your units in most newspapers daily, and when you do you will see the difference between the buying and selling prices, or the 'spread'. In time this will be probably replaced by a single price which is between the two.

You can sell your units simply and easily, as the unit trust company (known as the fund manager) has to buy back your units immediately if you wish to sell. You will receive the current 'bid' price (this is the lower of the prices quoted in the newspaper). If you want to buy you will pay the higher of the two prices, the 'offer' price, or you may be told that your purchase will be at the opening price tomorrow (known as forward pricing). Interest paid is called 'distributions' and is variable. It is made up of dividends received on the underlying investment. It is either paid twice yearly or can be automatically reinvested for you. In the latter case 'accumulation' units (the prices of which are higher than the income unit, reflecting the retention of the dividend income) are added to your stock of units. There is a growing trend to provide monthly income to unit-holders interested in this service. Interest is paid net of basic rate tax and you will receive a 'tax credit' voucher which you will need when you fill in your tax return. Although the unit trust itself is not liable to capital gains tax, any gains you make on your holdings in unit trusts will be subject to this tax over the current tax-free level.

Your investor protection comes at two levels – through the trustee who holds the assets in the fund, usually a major bank or insurance company, and under the provisions of the Financial Services Act where the investor compensation scheme provides cover up to a maximum of £48,000.

Buying and Selling: Through a financial adviser, stockbroker, bank, some building societies or direct from the company of your choice (but in this case you will not be able to benefit from the commission awarded to an adviser selling to you).

Upside: A good home for your long-term savings, offering reasonable security for investment in the equity markets.

Downside: You are being asked to take risks and should realise that the prices of unit trusts can go down as well as up, as can the income! The initial upfront charges are high, in the region of 5 per cent, and there is an annual management charge, generally some $1\frac{1}{2}$ per cent. You should remember, too, that there is a huge choice available and some unit trusts are riskier than others. If you read the objectives of the scheme for the unit trust in which you are interested this should help you to determine if you are looking at the right unit trust for you.

INVESTMENT TRUSTS

Like unit trusts these can also be seen as 'starter kits' for those who are interested in putting a toe into the equity markets. These are also collective investments, where your money is pooled with that of other investors, and invested in a profession-ally managed and well-spread portfolio of stocks and shares. An investment trust is a publicly quoted company and the shares are quoted on the Stock Exchange. They fall or rise in relation to the prevailing economic and market conditions. Sometimes they trade above what is called their 'net asset value', which means that they are trading at a premium. At other times are traded at a discount, which is when they are below their net asset value. Like unit trusts they are divided into different market and geographic sectors. You can also get investment trust PEPs and investment trust savings schemes, 'split' trusts and other special options, all of which are increas-ingly popular.

Investment trusts are suitable for anyone willing to take some risk and wanting long-term investment. Realistic minimums for lump sum investment are from £500, but regular savings plans are also available from £25 per month and charges are related to stockbrokers' commission rates. You can sell your shares at any time and in any amount. Interest is variable, and like shares it is called 'dividend income', usually paid half-yearly and net of basic rate tax.

Your investor protection is through the investors' compensa-tion scheme, to a maximum of £48,000, under the provisions of the Financial Services Act.

Buying and Selling: Through a stockbroker or your bank's share-dealing services or financial adviser.

Upside: You can enjoy real growth from your money in the good times and over the longer term. You also enjoy the skills of professional investment management. Costs are generally lower than for unit trusts. Another 'plus' factor is that the investment trust company is allowed to borrow money to invest, something not allowed to a unit trust company.

Downside: You are being asked to take risks, so the value of your holdings could go down, as well as up, as can your income.

SHARES (including the unlisted securities market)

Ordinary shares are investments quoted on the Stock Exchange. This means that the organisation concerned has qualified through a detailed vetting process which seeks to ensure that it is 'fit and proper' for people to invest their money in it, either directly or indirectly (through unit or investment trusts). Remember that share price is *not* related to the real value of the enterprise; it is really the price which the stockmarket thinks it can sell shares for. The shareholders of a company are one of a small group of important 'stakeholders' in that company and the objective of the firm's management is to try to deliver to you, as a shareholder, a rising share price as well as a satisfactory income on your investment through the payment of a dividend, or interest, on the money you invest. Shares have many uses, the most important of which, from a saver's point of view, is to help you to increase your capital, and to provide a satisfactory haven for long-term money if you are interested in long-term capital appreciation. Shares can be quite safe (although never entirely safe), and also very risky, depending on the company concerned, its potential and the quality of its management. It is vital to remember, when considering investment in the equity markets, that share prices can fall as well as rise, as many have found to their cost in the not too distant past!

Shareholders' 'perks' are a fairly recent innovation, providing lots of different goodies of many varieties to encourage you to invest in that company. You should consider these as useful extras, but never let them cloud your judgement in the selection of the company!

Shares are suitable for anyone who has sufficient spare cash to invest for the long term, and while there is in theory no lower limit in relation to buying shares it is sensible to consider parcels of shares of not less than £500. This is because the cost of dealing (buying and selling) has to be taken into account. Stockbrokers' fees are no longer fixed; some don't like small shareholders and those that do could have minimum fees of £20 and more for each transaction.

Income is variable and paid by way of dividends half-yearly. On rare occasions companies may suspend the payment of a dividend, so be on your guard. The dividends are paid net of basic rate tax, known as a 'tax credit'. Any gains over the annual exemption limit announced in the budget are, of course, liable for capital gains tax. You can withdraw from the market, in whole or in part, at any time.

Your investor protection is under the Financial Services Act, where the investors' compensation scheme covers up to £48,000. Don't forget, however, that this will not help you if your loss is as a result of the poor performance of the company or the fluctuations of the stock markets.

Buying and Selling: Through a bank's share-dealing services, a stockbroker or a financial adviser.

Upside: Your money could achieve major growth in good times, and with a good selection of shares, but you need to have enough money to hedge your bets and invest in reasonable amounts, of say, £2,000 and over, in at least ten to fifteen different equities.

Downside: You could lose every penny if the markets perform disastrously or if the company goes bust!

PERSONAL EQUITY PLANS

These are relatively new tax-efficient investment options for lump sums or regular savings. There is a limit of up to £6,000 each year invested in UK shares, or in companies on the unlisted securities market (the 'nursery' for smaller companies). PEPs are also allowed in relation to investments in unit and investment trusts. In this context the authorised and registered managers of the PEP (a bank, unit or investment trust or stockbroker) offer you a choice of a small number of one to ten shares, their share selection, and/or a mixture of unit and investment trusts. The attractions of PEPs mean that you qualify for tax concessions and your dividend or interest can be paid tax free. You are also allowed to invest £3,000 into a single-company PEP as well as your main PEP. PEPs are suitable for the long-term investor, and can be used for many purposes including school fees and retirement planning. They are suitable for anyone aged eighteen or over who has not already started a PEP that year. Minimums vary, generally £20 and over for a regular monthly saving PEP, and £250 for lump sum investment in a PEP. You can withdraw your money at any time. Interest is, of course, variable with the dividend being free of income tax, and all proceeds are free of capital gains tax.

PEPs should be viewed as tax-efficient, long-term investments. There is no point in considering a PEP if you pay no tax and if your resources are not sufficient to exceed the capital gains tax allowances! They are strictly for those belonging to the affluent and very affluent brigades!

Your investor protection is under the Financial Services Act. The investor's compensation scheme covers up to £48,000.

Buying and Selling: Through a bank, some building societies, unit or investment trust group offering PEPs.

Upside: Most people are attracted to PEPs by the preferential tax position.

Downside: In practice, many people have found that, when charges are taken into account, their performance has been less than golden in the recent past!

Variable capital, variable interest, variable currency

We have seen recently that currency values can be very volatile and can swing widely within very short periods. This is an area for the real 'professionals', but it can be attractive if you like taking serious risks in the hope of making serious money!

OFFSHORE

Currency funds
These are lump sum investments purchasing shares in a professionally managed fund based outside the UK. The fund invests

163

in a range of cash and other monetary investments in a variety of foreign currencies. It is based on judging that one currency will rise in value against others. Good for those when they get it right . . . but risky! Currency funds are suitable for those investors who want or need to hold their assets abroad. The benefits to UK-based investors are strictly limited. They are open to anyone aged eighteen or over and there is usually a minimum, in the region of £1,000. Charges are much in line with unit trusts, an initial fee and an annual maintenance fee. Interest is variable, paid either half-yearly or annually, paid gross, but if you are a UK taxpayer you have to declare interest and pay tax on it in the normal way. You will need to give seven days' notice of withdrawal.

Investor protection is complex and could be limited so find out exactly where you stand if you opt to invest in currency funds.

Buying and Selling: Mostly direct. Consult the *Financial Times* and other specialist financial media for information and take great care before you part with your money.

Upside: You could make a lot of money.

Downside: You could lose your shirt!

Unit trusts

Offshore unit trusts really work in the same way as UK authorised unit trusts, but, because the enterprise is based offshore, it comes under different regulations. If the fund is based in the Channel Islands or the Isle of Man, or even Bermuda, the funds operate under a system similar to the UK and a similar compensation scheme applies. If, however, the fund is offered by a Common Market country to investors in any EC Member State it has to conform to UCIT rules (Undertaking for Collective Investments in Transferable Securities). The rules are very similar to those in the UK, but there is no investors' compensation scheme to form a safety net for you as the investor.

Offshore unit trusts are suitable for those who wish to keep their foreign earnings assets in a foreign country or to transfer funds outside the UK. They are open to anyone and minimum investment is usually £500 or over. Charges are similar to UK unit trust charging structures, with an initial charge and an annual maintenance fee. You can usually withdraw on demand at the current market price, but you may have to give a month's notice depending on the company with which you are dealing. Interest is variable, paid as a dividend, gross, half-yearly. If you are a UK investor you have to declare interest received and pay tax on it in the usual way.

Your investor protection is likely to be non-existent so check up on this.

Buying and Selling: Direct. Check with the specialist financial publications such as *Financial Times* for details of management companies and prices.

Upside: You could make money.

Downside: You could lose out.

Variable capital, no interest

This is a further, glamorous area, for those with money, who like to take serious risks in the hope of making serious money! It is not recommended for the beginner, or the person who can't afford the 'gamble' involved if and when they lose.

GOLD

For a stake in gold the easiest route is to buy 'bullion-type' gold coins. Remember, though, that this provides no income for you. It is held purely for the possible growth in value that it could represent. Investing in gold is open to anyone, but it comes at a high price. A gold coin in today's markets could easily cost some £200. Commission charges can also be high. These are included in the price of the coin, also VAT at the current rate. Storage charges for your gold coins will also need to be paid, and a typical charge could be £2 a coin as well as an annual service fee of £1. You can withdraw your money by selling your stock of gold coins and get the current market rate immediately. There is, however, capital gains tax charged on any gain you make on and above the annual exemption limit announced in each year's budget and you will need to declare this on your tax return if you are a UK resident.

There is really no investor protection to help you . . . You're strictly on your own!

Buying and Selling: Most banks will buy and sell gold coins, but they will usually impose a minimum of ten coins.

Upside: You could be on to a good thing.

Downside: Your investment doesn't earn you interest or dividends of any sort and you could find the capital value goes down too.

ANTIQUES AND OTHER VALUABLES

These are some of the most pleasurable methods of investing your money. Today they include many more and modest 'collectables', from real cars to Dinky toys, teddy bears and stamps. They provide you with no income opportunities, but they do give you the practical benefit of being able to enjoy them in use every day. They can provide you with very attractive capital growth opportunities! Equally they can help to lose you your shirt! One factor to be borne well in mind is that there can be enormous mark-ups when you buy an antique or other valuable. It is common knowledge that insurance valuations are some 50 per cent up on what the item may fetch if it has to be sold. Beautiful things are of course a delight and joy to everyone, and so are suitable for anyone. Buying is easy, selling may be something else. To sell a beautiful or valuable item you must find a buyer. The value, ultimately, is what someone may be prepared to pay for the item in question. If you have to sell your beautiful item through someone else, you may be astonished to discover the level of the mark-up demanded. Do be very sure you know what you are doing before you buy or sell an antique or other valuable item as an investment. If, however, you do sell a valuable item at a price running into thousands of pounds, check up on your capital gains tax position to ensure that you don't get on the wrong side of the law!

Your investor protection is you!

Buying and Selling: Through reputable dealers and auctions, and privately, only if you really know what you are doing.

Upside: You get the pleasure of use and ownership, and the value of your investment could increase.

Downside: You could damage or destroy your investment through carelessness, bad luck etc. Also, the value of your investment could substantially decrease because of market conditions. You have the additional duty and cost of insuring your investment.

Other options of importance

HOME INCOME SCHEMES

Home income schemes have been much in the news recently. On a practical level, they offer you many advantages if you are elderly (say seventy or over) and want to boost your income.

The way the system works is that you get a loan based on the security of your home. This is used to buy an annuity from an insurance company to provide income for you during your lifetime – the company having naturally deducted from your income basic rate tax and the interest on their loan to you. When you die the loan is repaid from your estate. Sometimes this can be by the sale of the home. There are many variations in the schemes on offer. One type is called 'reversionary'. In this you actually sell all or part of your home to the company. In this case any increase in value is to their advantage, however if the value of the property falls it is their loss and not yours!

You get tax relief on the full amount of the loan interest provided under home income schemes if the loan is not more than £30,000. If you pay tax at more than the basic rate you can claim extra tax relief.

If you are thinking that a home income scheme may be of interest to you, be very, very careful. While there are many practical benefits, in volatile financial markets many have found that they have lost their homes because of the specific conditions in the particular scheme to which they enrolled.

Specifically, ensure that you know what you are doing if the money released to you is put into a bond or equity-related scheme to provide you with the income you have arranged. Many have found that they have been receiving their income through the erosion of their capital and have had to pay for the privilege in terms of remuneration to the adviser! This is because of the movement downwards in the equity markets of the time.

That is not to say that home income schemes do not have their place in the financial services market-place. Used properly they have much to offer. If you are considering a home income scheme, in particular look at the fine print in any reversionary and variable interest rate scheme. Remember, too, that purchasing an annuity is a one-way street; you can't change your mind or cancel it!

COMMODITIES AND FUTURES

These are options for you to consider if you really want to live dangerously in relation to your savings and investments.

Investing in commodities will certainly give your money a chance of growth over the long term, but you may need nerves of steel in the interim! Investment in commodities represents a high risk and *possibly* high return. So it is really only for those who understand what they are doing. Indeed, under the provisions of the Financial Services Act commodity brokers have to be specially careful as to whom they can accept as a suitable private investor.

There are two ways to invest in commodities: buying and selling commodities through a commodities broker; or through putting money into a special commodities fund. By contrast, investing in futures does not mean a long-term investment. It is essentially a gamble, on what will happen to the price of your chosen commodity over a relatively short time . . . Exciting it may be, for modest savers and investors it is not.

TIMESHARE

This a relatively new development for those who want to buy another property in the UK or abroad and haven't the where-withal! If you buy a timeshare you buy a specified number of weeks in the holiday home you have chosen over each year. There are opportunities which may be provided to you to 'swop' with others to vary the places you visit and also to change the dates which were initially agreed with you. The imponderables are many, and the system can work or not, largely depending on a lot of luck!

It is true to say that timeshares have been much in the news in the recent past because many who purchased them have found that there are snags which weren't too apparent at the time! These include the use of high-pressure selling techniques, the difficulty of selling without taking a large loss and problems of ensuring suitable arrangements for changing dates, proper maintenance of the property etc.

So, if you think timeshares are for you be very, very careful and examine all the fine print before you buy.

Worth special consideration

TERM ASSURANCE

Term assurance is one of the unsung heroes of the insurance world. It is simple, practical, easy and reasonable. Essentially, you insure for an agreed period, at the rate and over the term you have agreed. If you die before the end of the 'term' specified in the policy the insurance company pays out. If you don't, at the end of the term you won't get any of your money back. But, essentially, at the reasonable rate you have been asked to pay, you have in exchange achieved peace of mind.

For a given amount of cover, term assurance is very much cheaper than other types of life insurance. There are other options in term assurance you can consider, for example, provision of a tax-free income instead of a lump sum if you die within the term. This type of policy is known as a family income benefit policy.

Term assurance very definitely has a more important role to play in effective money management for those with dependants than is generally acknowledged.

REPAYMENT MORTGAGE

This is the most common type of mortgage. You pay a monthly amount which is fixed, unless the mortgage interest rate changes. This amount is part capital (the sum borrowed) and part interest. In the first few years most of the monthly repayment goes in interest and only a little pays off the capital. There is tax relief currently up to £30,000.

(Note: Today the mortgage market is very sophisticated and, if you are buying a home, it will pay you to study the different mortgage options carefully before you take a decision. In past years a home has proved to be a very good investment, but over the recent past many have found that house prices can go down as well as up. In a book on savings and investments it is important to consider buying a house more in terms of responsibility for taking up a major loan than as a sure-fire option in terms of investment! However, it must be said that owning your own home does offer other advantages in addition to a possible increase in value, and this needs also to be taken into consideration.)

Appendix

Sources of help and information

Regulatory organisations

Securities and Investments Board (SIB) – the 'lead' regulator
Gavrelle House, 2–14 Bunhill Row, London EC1Y 8RA   Tel:
071-638 1240. Central Register   Tel: 071-929 3652

Financial Intermediaries, Managers and Brokers Regulatory
Association (FIMBRA) – regulating financial advisers in the
independent sector
Hertsmere House, Hertsmere Road, London E14 4AB   Tel:
071-538 8860

Investment Management Regulatory Organisation (IMRO) –
regulating corporate investment management companies and
advisers, including pension fund managers, unit trust managers
and some banks
Broadwalk House, 6 Appold Street, London EC2A 2AA   Tel:
071-628 6022

Life Assurance and Unit Trust Regulatory Organisation
(LAUTRO) – regulating the marketing of insurance companies,
unit trusts and friendly societies
Centre Point, 103 New Oxford Street, London WC1A 1QH
Tel: 071-379 0444

Securities and Futures Authority (SFA) – regulating members

of the Stock Exchange, dealers in international stocks and money market investments, and advisers, managers and dealers in futures and options
Cotton Centre, Cottons Lane, London SE1 2QB   Tel: 071-378 9000

Note: Personal Investment Authority (PIA) - this new retail regulator for private investors, at the time of writing, will commence operating in mid 1994. In due course this will mean the closure of LAUTRO and FIMBRA whose activity will be taken over by PIA.
3-4 Royal Exchange Buildings, London EC3V 3NL   Tel: 071-929 0072

Recognised Professional Bodies (RPBs)

There are many organisations qualifying as RPBs, of which the following are the most used by private savers and investors:

Institute of Chartered Accountants in England and Wales (ICEAW)
PO Box 433, Chartered Accountants' Hall, Moorgate Place, London EC2P 2BJ   Tel: 071-920 8100

Institute of Chartered Accountants in Ireland
Chartered Accountants House, 87–9 Pembroke Road, Dublin 4   Tel: 010-3531 680400

Institute of Chartered Accountants of Scotland
27 Queen Street, Edinburgh EH2 1LA   Tel: 031-225 5673

Insurance Brokers Registration Council (IBRC)
15 St Helen's Place, London EC3A 6DS   Tel: 071-588 4387

The Law Society
113 Chancery Lane, London WC2A 1PL   Tel: 071-242 1222

The Law Society of Northern Ireland
Law Society House, 98 Victoria Street, Belfast BT1 3JZ   Tel: 0232 231614

The Law Society of Scotland
Law Society Hall, 26 Drumsheugh Gardens, Edinburgh
EH3 7YR   Tel: 031-226 7411

The Investors' Compensation Scheme

Gavrelle House, 2–14 Bunhill Row, London EC1Y 8RA   Tel:
071-628 8820

Ombudsman Schemes and other complaints procedures

The Insurance Ombudsman
City Gate One, 135 Park Street, London SE1 9EA   Tel:
071-928 4488

The Office of the Banking Ombudsman
70 Grays Inn Road, London WC1X 8NB   Tel: 071-404 9944

The Building Societies Ombudsman
Grosvenor Gardens House, 35–7 Grosvenor Gardens, London
SW1X 7AW   Tel: 071-931 0044

The Investment Ombudsman
6 Fredericks Place, London EC2R 8BT   Tel: 071-796 3065

The Pensions Ombudsman
11 Belgrave Road, London SW1V 1RB   Tel: 071-834 9144

Advisory, Conciliation and Arbitration Service
Clifton House, 83 Euston Road, London NW1   Tel: 071-388
5100

Note: Personal Investment Authority Ombudsman Bureau - at
the time of writing it is considered that this scheme will be
introduced in mid 1994, with the introduction of PIA.
3-4 Royal Exchange Buildings, London EC3V 3NL Tel:
071-929 0072

Consumer organisations

Consumers' Association
2 Marylebone Road, London NW1 4DF   Tel: 071-486 5544

The National Federation of Consumer Groups
12 Mosley Street, Newcastle upon Tyne NE1 1DE Tel: 091-261 8259

The National Consumer Council
20 Grosvenor Gardens, London SW1W 0DH   Tel: 071-730 3469

Independent Banking Advisory Service (IBAS)
North View, North Fen, Somersham, Huntingdon, Cambs. PE17 3HW   Tel: 0487 843444

Trade and professional associations

The British Bankers Association
10 Lombard Street, London EC3V 9EL   Tel: 071-623 4001

The Association of British Insurers
51 Gresham Street, London EC2V 7HQ   Tel: 071-600 3333

The Building Societies Association
3 Savile Row, London W1X 1AF   Tel: 071-437 0655

The Council of Mortgage Lenders
3 Savile Row, London W1X 1AF   Tel: 071-437 0655

The Life Insurance Association
Citadel House, Station Approach, Chorleywood, Rickmansworth, Hertfordshire WD3 5PF   Tel: 0923 285333

The Association of Unit Trusts and Investment Funds
65 Kingsway, London WC2B 6TD   Tel: 071-831 0898

The Association of Investment Trust Companies
Park House (6th Floor), 16 Finsbury Circus, London EC2M 7JJ   Tel: 071-588 5347

Proshare UK Ltd
Library Chambers, 13–14 Basinghall Street, London EC2V
5BQ Tel: 071-600 0984

The British Insurance and Investment Brokers Association
14 Bevis Marks, London EC3A 7NT Tel: 071-623 9043

The National Federation of Independent Financial Advisers
Riverlock House, Spring Gardens Road, High Wycombe, Bucks
HP13 7AG Tel: 0494 473018

IFAP (Independent Financial Advice Promotion)
28 Greville Street, London EC1N 8SU Tel: 071-831 4027

Student Loan Company Ltd

100 Bothwell Street, Glasgow G2 7JD
Tel: 041-306 2000

Office of Fair Trading

Field House, 15–25 Breams Buildings, London EC4A 1PR
Tel: 071-242 2858

Helpful newspaper columns, radio and television programmes and magazines

Money Mail (Wednesdays) *The Times* (Saturdays) *Observer* (Sundays) *Sunday Telegraph* (Sundays) *Mail on Sunday* (Sundays) *Daily Telegraph* (weekdays) *Financial Times* (weekdays and Saturdays)

Money Box and *Money Box Live* (BBC Radio 4), *Watchdog* (BBC 1)

Moneywise (monthly) *Which?* (monthly) *Investor's Chronicle* (monthly)

Weekly financial trade papers
Financial Adviser Tel: 071-608 3471

Money Marketing Tel: 071-287 5678

Consumer Information on Personal Finance

The Money Management Council, PO Box 77, Hertford, Herts
SG14 2HW   Tel: 0992 503448

Glossary / Money Jargon

Annuity A form of life assurance that, like a pension, provides for a sum of money to be paid to you at regular intervals if you have bought a policy for a lump sum.

Arrears What you owe, the amount due for payment under an agreement.

Assets What you own. These may include the money values of your house, car, furniture and its equivalent, such as your investments and savings (called 'liquid assets' because you can spend them) and special skills or the goodwill of, for example, a business which you may own (called 'intangible assets' because you use them to earn money).

Assurance An arrangement by which something is promised or guaranteed. The word most commonly appears in the term 'life assurance' which means that money will be paid on death.

Bears (on the Stock Exchange) Pessimistic investors who believe share prices will fall.

Bid price (of unit trusts) The price which the unit trust management company will pay for the units you sell back to it.

Broker An agent who, in return for commission, buys or sells goods, securities, insurance etc.

Bulls (on the Stock Exchange) Investors who take an optimistic view that share prices will rise.

Commission   Money usually paid to employees, agents or financial advisers for selling you products such as endowments, pensions and unit trusts.

Completion   When purchasing (or selling), the final date on which the necessary documents take effect with transfer of ownership.

Contracted out (of SERPS)   When you opt to leave the State Pension Scheme to go into a private one.

Disclosure   Requirements to reveal fee or commission payments to you as the purchaser of a financial services product or service.

Endowment   A policy which ensures you a guaranteed fixed sum at maturity or death, if earlier.

Equities   The 'ordinary shares' of a limited company which entitle holders to a share of the profits and of the company's assets after all the liabilities have been met.

Equity   The goodwill and assets of a company after all liabilities have been deducted. Also the interest of an 'ordinary' shareholder in a company (*see* Equities).

Executor   The person appointed to carry out the terms of a dead person's will.

Face value   The apparent value, printed or written, on any document such as a £10 note or a bond. The market value is not always the face value.

Financial Services Act 1986   The legislation which created self-regulatory authorities to control the management, marketing and sales of financial services products.

Fringe benefits   Payments in kind, or what an employee gets on top of regular earnings from an employer, such as a company car, medical insurance or meal vouchers.

Gilt   Abbreviation for 'gilt edged' – highest quality securities in the UK. The term normally applies only to Government

Stocks which are gilt-edged as there is virtually no default attached to them.

Gilt trust A unit trust launched specially to invest in UK government gilt-edged securities.

Indemnity (i) A guaranteed compensation for loss. (ii) It can also mean the legal exemption from liabilities resulting from your actions or defaults.

Independent Advisers who are not tied or obliged to recommend the products of a particular company.

Insurance A service that offers a policyholder financial protection against specified events (such as death, loss or damage to property) that may or may not occur.

Interest Amount charged for the use of credit or borrowed money. Also known as a 'service charge'.

Interest rate A percentage charged for borrowing money, usually so many per cent per year.

Investment trusts Closed-end collective investments whose shares are quoted on the London Stock Exchange.

Junk bonds Originating from the USA, these are high interest stock offered by companies with a low credit rating, therefore considered as a high risk to investors.

Liquidity Cash or assets which you can turn into cash.

Market value The amount that can be got on the open, competitive market for the sale of an asset.

Money purchase scheme A pension policy where the benefits paid out are based on the amount of contributions paid in and the performance of their investment.

Occupational pension The name given to a company's (or other business organisation's) pension scheme.

Offshore fund A fund established outside the UK (the UK in this case being taken to exclude the Channel Islands and the Isle of Man). These funds are run on broad unit trust principles, but are not authorised or controlled by the Department of Trade and Industry. They vary in their adherence to the standards of UK unit trust practice.

PEP (personal equity plan) PEPs were introduced in the 1986 Budget to encourage wider share ownership. Dividends (income) and capital gains on shares (whether equities, investment or unit trust holdings) are exempt from income and capital gains taxes. Withdrawals from PEPs are tax free.

Plan manager These are the persons or companies authorised to make investments on your behalf. They must be members of a recognised professional or regulatory body, such as FIMBRA (for independent advisers) or IMRO (for investment managers). The plan manager makes all the claims for your tax reliefs and exemptions to the Inland Revenue, and also for ensuring that the plan is within the rules of the scheme. The Inland Revenue will also tell you whether a particular plan manager is approved.

Portfolio An investment term for all the securities belonging to any one person.

Premium (i) In insurance the premium is the amount you pay, usually in regular instalments, for your insurance policy. (ii) The amount you pay above the normal price level. This may reflect current market conditions.

'Pushing' shares Talking enthusiastically about a share so that its price rises.

Rat race The blind pursuit of success.

Rebate An allowance or refund against the cost of a service, subject to agreement.

Redundancy The term used to mean that the job itself is disappearing and therefore there is no future need for your services.

Share exchange schemes Where such a scheme exists, you can exchange numerous small holdings in various companies or trusts (for example ones you bought in privatisation issues) according to the terms of the individual scheme. Some scheme managers offer free share exchange services or services on very competitive terms.

SERPS (State Earnings Related Pension Scheme)   This enables the employee to an 'earnings related' pension equivalent to a set amount of relevant earnings up to a maximum of twenty years.

Speculation   Gambling or buying, in the hope of making a financial gain.

Tax avoidance   Legal avoidance of taxes. For instance, you can legally avoid paying tax on articles you buy entirely for business use, if this satisfies the current rules laid down by the Inland Revenue.

Tax evasion   The illegal evasion of paying tax.

Tied agent   The agent or company restricted to selling the products or services of only one company.

Unit-linked plan   A life assurance policy under which the premiums paid are invested in a unit-linked insurance fund or a unit trust. Its value fluctuates with the current price of the units.

Unit trusts   Open-ended funds formed to manage investments collectively on behalf of a number of investors under terms and conditions laid out in the specific trust.

Unlisted securities   These are private companies and those organisations which have not been through the official Stock Exchange procedures to become fully registered as 'listed companies'.

Whole life policy   An assurance policy that pays out a sum insured only on death.

Yield   The phrase used to express the annual return from an investment.

Bibliography

The Money Guide (*The Money Jungle*), Marie Jennings, Collins, 1983

Women and Money, Marie Jennings, Penguin Books, 1988

Which? Way to Save and Invest, Hodder & Stoughton, 1993

Daily Mail Savers' Guide 1992/3, Chapman, 1992

Daily Mail Income Tax 1992/1993, Chapman, 1992

The Instant Investor, E. B. Groves, Letts, 1991

The Allied Dunbar Investment and Savings Guide 1991/1992, Longman, 1991

Earning Money in Retirement, Kenneth Lyons, Age Concern, 1992

Investing in Shares, Hugh Pym and Nick Kochan, Longman, 1988

Financial Planning for the Individual, Alan Kelly, *Financial Times* Business Information, 1989

Perfectly Legal Tax Loopholes, Courtney, Piatkus (revised edition)

Index

PIATKUS BUSINESS BOOKS

Piatkus Business Books have been created for people who need expert knowledge readily available in a clear and easy-to-follow format. All the books are written by specialists in their field. They will help you improve your skills quickly and effortlessly in the workplace and on a personal level.

Titles include:

Financial Planning

Great Boom Ahead, The Harry Dent
How to Choose Stockmarket Winners Raymond Caley
Perfectly Legal Tax Loopholes Stephen Courtney

Careers and Training

How to Find the Perfect Job Tom Jackson
Marketing Yourself: How to sell yourself and get the jobs you've always wanted Dorothy Leeds
Networking and Mentoring: A woman's guide Dr Lily M. Segerman-Peck
Perfect CV, The Tom Jackson
Perfect Job Search Strategies Tom Jackson
Secrets of Successful Interviews Dorothy Leeds
Sharkproof: Get the job you want, keep the job you love in today's tough job market Harvey Mackay
10-Day MBA, The Steven Silbiger
Ten Steps To The Top Marie Jennings
Which Way Now? How to plan and develop a successful career Bridget Wright

Presentation and Communication

Better Business Writing Maryann V. Piotrowski
Complete Book of Business Etiquette, The Lynne Brennan and David Block
Confident Conversation Dr Lillian Glass
Confident Speaking: How to communicate effectively using the

Power Talk System Christian H. Godefroy and Stephanie Barrat

He Says, She Says: Closing the communication gap between the sexes Dr Lillian Glass

Personal Power Philippa Davies

Powerspeak: The complete guide to public speaking and presentation Dorothy Leeds

Presenting Yourself: A personal image guide for men Mary Spillane

Presenting Yourself: A personal image guide for women Mary Spillane

Say What You Mean and Get What You Want George R. Walther

Your Total Image Philippa Davies

Self-Improvement

Brain Power: The 12-week mental training programme Marilyn vos Savant and Leonore Fleischer

Creating Abundance Andrew Ferguson

Creative Thinking Michael LeBoeuf

Memory Booster: Easy techniques for rapid learning and a better memory Robert W. Finkel

Organise Yourself Ronni Eisenberg with Kate Kelly

Quantum Learning: Unleash the genius within you Bobbi DePorter with Mike Hernacki

Right Brain Manager, The: How to use the power of your mind to achieve personal and professional success Dr Harry Alder

Three Minute Meditator, The David Harp with Nina Feldman

General Management and Business Skills

Beware the Naked Man Who Offers You His Shirt Harvey Mackay

Be Your Own PR Expert: The complete guide to publicity and public relations Bill Penn

Complete Conference Organiser's Handbook, The Robin O'Connor

Complete Time Management System, The Christian H. Godefroy and John Clark

Confident Decision Making J. Edward Russo and Paul J. H. Schoemaker

Energy Factor, The: How to motivate your workforce Art McNeil

Firing On All Cylinders: The quality management system for high-powered corporate performance Jim Clemmer with Barry Sheehy

How to Collect the Money You Are Owed Malcolm Bird

How to Implement Corporate Change John Spencer and Adrian Pruss

Influential Manager, The: How to develop a powerful management style Lee Bryce

Leadership Skills for Every Manager Jim Clemmer and Art McNeil

Lure the Tiger Out of the Mountains: Timeless tactics from the East for today's successful manager Gao Yuan

Managing Your Team John Spencer and Adrian Pruss

Outstanding Negotiator, The Christian H. Godefroy and Luis Robert

Problem Solving Techniques That Really Work Malcolm Bird

Seven Cultures of Capitalism, The: Value systems for creating wealth in Britain, the United States, Germany, France, Japan, Sweden and the Netherlands Charles Hampden-Turner and Fons Trompenaars

Smart Questions for Successful Managers Dorothy Leeds

Strategy of Meetings, The George David Kieffer

Sales and Customer Services

Art of the Hard Sell, The Robert L. Shook

Creating Customers David H. Bangs

Guerrilla Marketing Excellence Jay Conrad Levinson

How to Close Every Sale Joe Girard

How to Make Your Fortune Through Network Marketing John Bremner

How to Succeed in Network Marketing Leonard Hawkins

How to Win Customers and Keep Them for Life Michael LeBoeuf

Sales Power: The Silva Mind Method for sales professionals José Silva and Ed Bernd Jr

Selling Edge, The Patrick Forsyth
Telephone Selling Techniques That Really Work Bill Good
Winning New Business: A practical guide to successful sales presentations Dr David Lewis

Personnel and People Skills

Best Person for the Job, The Malcolm Bird
Dealing with Difficult People Roberta Cava
Problem Employees: How to improve their behaviour and their performance Peter Wylie and Mardy Grothe
Psychological Testing for Managers Dr Stephanie Jones

Motivational

Play to Your Strengths Donald O. Clifton and Paula Nelson
Winning Edge, The Charles Templeton

Small Business

How to Run a Part-Time Business Barrie Hawkins
Making Profits: a six-month plan for the small business Malcolm Bird
Profit Through the Post: How to set up and run a successful mail order business Alison Cork

For a free brochure with further information on our complete range of business titles, please write to:

Piatkus Books
Freepost 7 (WD 4505)
London W1E 4EZ

PIATKUS